for Germain Grisez

Lord of
the elves
and eldils

Richard L. Purtill

Lord of the elves and eldils

fantasy and philosophy in c·s· Lewis and J·R·R· tolkien

By
Richard Purtill

ZONDERVAN
PUBLISHING HOUSE
OF THE ZONDERVAN CORPORATION
GRAND RAPIDS. MICHIGAN 49506

This book is dedicated to

J. R. R. TOLKIEN

*in gratitude for the many hours
of enchantment I have received
from his work since as a boy
I first took The Hobbit
from a library shelf.*

Contents

Acknowledgments

My thanks are due to the National Endowment for the Humanities for a summer grant which enabled me to do some of the research and writing for this book and to the Research Office of Western Washington State College, both for travel grants which enabled me to visit the C. S. Lewis Collection at Wheaton College and also for the typing of the manuscript. Special thanks to Mrs. Ann Drake, who typed the manuscript, to Professor Clyde Kilby at Wheaton for many kindnesses, and to T. A. Bryant, Gerard Terpstra, and James E. Ruark of the Zondervan Publishing House.

Introduction

In this book I write about the ideas and imaginings
of two men. The men are C. S. Lewis and J. R. R.
Tolkien, and their books range from fantasies, some
highly popular, to scholarly works of little interest
except to specialists in their fields. Both men taught
at Oxford and they met regularly, with or without
other friends, over a period of years, both for conversation and conviviality and to read to each other
their work in progress. They agreed on many matters,
not the least on religion, and on a general attitude toward literature and life. One perceptive observer and
sometime junior member of their circle described
them as having "a corporate mind, as all effective
groups must," and there is at least an element of
truth in this. But in other respects they were almost
comically dissimilar, and their shared assumptions were
expressed in very different ways.

One important way in which their books are alike
is that both found it best to create for the purposes of
their fiction to other worlds — not utopias or dystopias
but *different* worlds — what Tolkien was to call
"secondary worlds." This sort of writing raises certain
little discussed problems, which this book explores.
Both also wrote *about* literature or at least about

certain aspects of it. Tolkien, who was primarily a philologist, did very little of this sort of writing, but what he did do was original and suggestive. Lewis, whose professional field was English literature, of course wrote a great deal on such subjects, some of it highly specialized but all worth reading. Part of my task in this book is to examine the ideas expressed by my authors on these subjects, ideas which are often in disagreement with the prevailing orthodoxy. I seek to weigh the consistency and defensibility of these ideas and also to see to what extent they are applicable to my authors' own writings.

Since I am a philosopher by profession, my interest in these authors is primarily in their ideas, not only in their ideas about literature but in their ethical and religious ideas and their views about language. Where these views are implicit in a work, I will try to make them explicit; where they are stated rather than argued for, I will try to see how they might be criticized and defended.

I know no more of the personal lives of my authors than can be found in the books written by or about them, and available to anyone, so it has not seemed worthwhile merely to summarize such secondhand information in this book. Somewhat more complicated is the question of whether to summarize those of their books which I discuss. While it is doubtful whether many people will be interested in a discussion of Lewis and Tolkien who have not read at least some of their work, some of my readers may have read Tolkien but not Lewis or vice versa. I have concluded that any adequate summary of the works I am interested in would take an inordinate amount of space and be a poor substitute for reading the works themselves.

Thus I presume at least some familiarity with the fictional works of both Lewis and Tolkien. A reader who lacks such familiarity would do well to stop here and read the works listed in the "essential" section of the Basic Lewis-Tolkien Bibliography (Appendix A).

Since I have hopes that this book will be of some interest both to scholars of Lewis and Tolkien and to ordinary readers, I have tried to reach a workable compromise between the pedantic accuracy of reference of a scholarly book and the less rigorous standards of a popular book. Thus, instead of citing the first publication of a book, I have usually cited the cheapest and most accessible edition, generally a paperback. When I refer to the same book a number of times, I give its title in full the first time I cite it, and if it is not one of the "essential" books from the bibliography, I give the usual publication information. Thereafter I refer to it by an abbreviated version of its title as I am discussing it. When I discuss the same book again in another chapter or after considerable discussion of other matters, I cite the title again in full but omit publication data. I hope this will be neither too pedantic for the common reader nor too lacking in rigour for the scholar.

In Appendix B I say something about those who have influenced my authors and a little about those who have been influenced by them. But I also take a critical look at the whole idea of the importance of "influences" which bulks so large in most writing about literature. I also say something about critics of Tolkien and Lewis, but not in the sense of a formal "reply to the critics." To tell the truth, very few of Tolkien's critics deserve a formal reply, and very few of Lewis's need one. Rather, I have used the critics as taking-off points for my own discussions. But if this book can provoke a better critic to do better what I have tried to do, to correct my misunderstandings and replace them with better interpretations, I will be quite happy.

The great importance of my authors, it seems to me, is that they have succeeded in restating certain traditional values, including traditional religious values, in such a way that they make an imaginative appeal to a very wide audience, young and old, traditionalist and untraditionalist. The wide appeal of Tolkien's *Lord of the Rings* trilogy on college campuses is perhaps the most striking example of this, but Lewis's fantasies have a similar audience.

Those who look with gloom at the contemporary scene (and who can avoid a certain amount of gloom at what is to be seen) often fall into one of two groups. The first group declares that old values have failed us and we must create new ones. The second group, to which my authors belong, declares that values are not the sort of thing which can be created. Certain values exist whether we will or not, and to these values we must conform or perish. To enable people to see these values and love them is the task to which Lewis and Tolkien set themselves. Their methods were unconventional; their success, though partial, was real.

Literature
and Language

chapter 1

Why Fantasy?

Those who enjoy reading and discussing Lewis and Tolkien often encounter an impatient, even irritated, reaction from friends or acquaintances. Why read fantasies or fairy-stories? Aren't such things for children? Shouldn't grown-ups read about "real life"? (One literary critic called Tolkien's trilogy a "children's story which got out of hand.") A former student of Lewis, novelist and critic John Wain, once challenged Lewis's own praise and enjoyment of fantasy.

A writer's task, I maintained, was to lay bare the human heart, and this could not be done if he were continually taking refuge in the spinning of fanciful webs. Lewis retorted with a theory that, since the Creator had seen fit to build a universe and set it in motion, it was the duty of the human artist to create as lavishly as possible in his turn. The romancer, who invents a whole world, is worshipping God more effectively than the mere realist who analyses that which lies about him. Looking back across fourteen years, I can hardly believe that Lewis said anything so manifestly absurd as this, and perhaps I misunderstood him; but that, at any rate, is how my memory reports the incident. [1]

---

[1] John Wain, *Sprightly Running. Part of an Autobiography* (New York: St. Martin's Press, 1963), p. 182.

Here we have very neatly the whole basis of the conflict between Lewis and Tolkien on the one hand and many modern writers and critics on the other. Wain maintains, and many moderns would agree, that a writer's task is to "lay bare the human heart." Judged by this standard, practically nothing written by Tolkien and only a few things written by Lewis carry out "the writer's task." The theory attributed to Lewis, which is a recognizable caricature of the theory developed by Tolkien in his essay "On Fairy-Stories," is dismissed as "manifestly absurd." Before discussing who is more nearly right, let us first try to understand more thoroughly the theory proposed by Lewis to Wain.

The theory, presumably, is that espoused by Tolkien in his essay, "On Fairy-Stories." According to Tolkien,

> the story-maker proves a successful "sub-creator." He makes a Secondary World which your mind can enter. Inside it, what he relates is "true": it accords with the laws of the world. You therefore believe it while you are, as it were, inside. [2]

This could be said of other forms of writing, but fantasy has special characteristics.

> The achievement of the expression, which gives (or seems to give) "the inner consistency of reality," is . . . Art, the operative link between Imagination and the final result, Sub-creation. For my present purpose I require a word which shall embrace both the Sub-creative Art in itself and a quality of strangeness and wonder in the Expression, derived from the Image: a quality essential to fairy-story. I propose . . . to use Fantasy for this purpose. . . . Fantasy (in this sense) is, I think, not a lower but a higher form of Art, indeed the most nearly pure form, and so (when achieved) the most potent. [3]

[2] *Tree and Leaf* in *The Tolkien Reader* (New York: Ballantine Books, 1966), p. 37.
[3] Ibid., p. 47.

Note several things to begin with. First, this is a theory about one kind of writing. Tolkien indeed suggests that it may, if properly handled, be the "most potent" form of narrative art or story-making. But this is not to say that it is the only allowable form even of narrative art, much less the only allowable form of writing. Wain, on the other hand, seems to suggest that the purpose of all "writing" (presumably by "writing" he means primarily "fiction") is to lay bare the secrets of the human heart. Second, the two views are not necessarily in conflict, even considered at their most extreme. One might consistently hold both that the purpose of fiction is to lay bare the secrets of the human heart and that the "most potent" way of doing this is to create a "secondary world" in Tolkien's sense.

This could be done in various ways. In strict allegory (e.g., Bunyan's *Pilgrim's Progress*) every figure, incident, or place in your secondary world will stand for some person, emotion, or idea in the primary world. In a well-worked-out strict allegory it should be possible to say what each person, place, or incident "stands for" (its *significatio*), and the whole story could be retold without the use of a secondary world (though it would lose something by this, or the allegory is useless).

In a loose allegory, on the other hand, it is impossible to find a *significatio* for each person, place, or incident, but the secondary world as a whole is intended to give a general impression or idea — for example, an idea of "the human condition." (Kafka and Beckett are good examples.) A work may be classified as loose allegory if the author seems to be saying, or trying to make us say, "That is what life is like."

With illustrative fantasy the author wishes to make a point about some aspect of the primary world which can best be made by isolating or exaggerating certain aspects of that world by the use of a secondary world (as in Golding's *Lord of the Flies*). The author of illustrative fantasy is saying, "This couldn't happen, of course, but if it did, this is how people would behave."

But there is a fourth use of secondary worlds which does not seem suited to "laying bare the heart." In appreciative fantasy (for example, *Alice in Wonderland*), the secondary world is enjoyed purely for its own sake. The characters, places, and incidents do not have a *significatio*, do not "stand for" anything in the primary world. The secondary world is not intended to show what "life is like," and there is no attempt to show that people would behave in a certain way given certain improbable occurrences. So although the first three of these sorts of allegory and fantasy can be used to "lay bare the secrets of the heart," this last sort of fantasy seems unsuited to that purpose. To write appreciative fantasy is, in fact, to "spin fanciful webs."

Now Lewis and Tolkien do not in the main write strict allegory or even loose allegory, nor do they write illustrative fantasy.[4] By their own statements, they aim at writing purely appreciative fantasy. Legolas the elf or Tumnus the faun have no *significatio*, illustrate no possible or plausible reaction of human nature, no views of what life is like. Tolkien writes about Legolas, Lewis about Tumnus, because they enjoy contemplating elves and fauns. They like to think about them and write about them. If such tastes were to disqualify them as "significant" writers, they would be undisturbed. They would rather write about Faëry than about "modern problems." And why not, if they and others enjoy it?

May we then merely say "laying bare the secrets of

---

[4] The exception for Lewis is *The Pilgrim's Regress*, a strict allegory, and for Tolkien "Leaf by Niggle," a loose allegory contained in *Tree and Leaf*.

18

the human heart" is one legitimate purpose of literature and the creation of secondary worlds is another? I fear that reconciliation is not likely to be so easy. For Wain, the creator of secondary worlds is "taking refuge in the spinning of fanciful webs." Tolkien's reply to this is that

> fantasy is a natural human activity. It certainly does not destroy or even insult reason; and it does not either blunt the appetite for, nor obscure the perception of, scientific verity. On the contrary, the keener and the clearer is the reason, the better fantasy will it make. . . . For creative Fantasy is founded upon the hard recognition that things are so in the world as it appears under the sun; on a recognition of fact, but not a slavery to it. [5]

Of course, fantasy, like everything else, can be abused.

> Fantasy can, of course, be carried to excess. It can be ill done. It can be put to evil uses. It may even delude the minds out of which it came. But of what human thing in this fallen world is that not true? Men have conceived not only of elves, but they have imagined gods, and worshipped them, even worshipped those most deformed by their authors' own evil. But they have made false gods out of other materials: their notions, their banners, their monies; even their sciences and their social and economic theories have demanded human sacrifice. *Abusus non tollit usum.* Fantasy remains a human right: we make in our measure and in our derivative mode, because we are made: and not only made, but made in the image and likeness of a Maker. [6]

What Tolkien says here is connected with his theory about the uses of fantasy, which is to say the uses of creating secondary worlds. In his view fantasy has three purposes: Recovery, Escape, and Consolation. By Re-

[5] *Tree and Leaf,* loc. cit., pp. 54-55.
[6] Ibid., p. 55.

covery he means a "regaining of a clear view . . . 'seeing things as we are (or were) meant to see them'" (p. 57). Familiarity has dulled our sense of the wonder and mystery of things; fantasy restores it. "You will be warned that all you had (or knew) was dangerous and potent, not really effectively chained, free and wild; no more yours than they were you."[7]

Notice that this implies two things. First, that many of us fail to see any wonder and mystery in things, which is undeniable. Second, that in so failing we are failing to see the truth, and this I suppose some would dispute.

By Escape Tolkien means nothing especially original. We must define Escape as the turning of our thoughts and affections away from what is around us to something else — the past, the future, a secondary world. Tolkien's originality lies in defending Escape when so many have deprecated it. His reasons are several. First, the modern world is preeminently something which it is desirable to escape *from*. "Why should a man be scorned if, finding himself in prison, he tries to get out and go home? Or if, when he cannot do so, he thinks and talks about other topics than jailers and prison-walls?"[8] And the modern world is, to Tolkien, prisonlike: ugly, cruel, and unjust.

A deeper reason for Escape, however, is the human longing to flee from our limitations. First is the hardness of life even at its best; but beyond this is our isolation from each other and from the living world around us. Finally, the great limit, Death, is something which men have tried to escape from in many fashions.

Here Tolkien's discussion of Escape merges into a discussion of the third use of fantasy. Consolation is

---

[7] Ibid., p. 59.
[8] Ibid., p. 60

20

secondarily the imaginative satisfaction of ancient desires, such as the desire to really communicate with species other than our own. But primarily it centers on the happy ending, the "eucatastrophe," the "sudden joyous 'turn'" (p. 68). This Consolation arises from the denial of "universal final defeat and in so far is *evangelium*, giving a fleeting glimpse of Joy, Joy beyond the walls of the world, poignant as grief" (p. 68).

In fantasy we have a happy ending, a joyous "turn" within the secondary world, to which we give secondary belief, and it gives such consolation as such things may, which is a good worth seeking. But Tolkien concludes by discussing the "Christian Story" as "a story of a larger kind which·embraces all the essence of fairy-stories" (p. 71). This is a eucatastrophe in the primary world, a happy ending to which primary belief can be given. Such belief leads to true Consolation. "There is no tale ever told that men would rather find was true, and none which so many skeptical men have accepted as true in its own merits. For the Art of it has the supremely convincing tone of Primary Art, that is, of Creation. To reject it leads either to sadness or to wrath." [9]

So we see in the end that Tolkien's view of fairy-stories is not just a view about literature, but a view about life. Tolkien could, if he liked, use Wain's formula about "laying bare the secrets of the human heart." But Tolkien would not agree with Wain or with most moderns on what those secrets are. For in Tolkien's view the important secret of the human heart is this longing for the real happy ending. And the most important thing about this longing is that it can be satisfied.

Indeed, no matter how "pure," how "appreciative" in our sense, a fantasy is, it is bound to reflect to some

---

[9] Ibid., p. 72.

extent the views or ideas of its writer, for several reasons. Lewis and Tolkien create secondary worlds. Because they are Christians, because they are British, even because they are Oxford dons, they create different secondary worlds than they otherwise might have.

For, of course, the sort of secondary world you create will depend on the sort of things you believe possible. Not scientifically possible, however — a secondary world may often have scientific laws quite different from those of the primary world — but what we might call "morally possible." Orwell could write *Nineteen Eighty-Four* because, although he didn't *want* such a state of affairs to be true, he thought such a state of affairs was "morally possible" in my sense. "A heel pressing down on the neck of Man — forever" was a real possibility for Orwell. But for many humanists as well as theists, such a fate for man is unthinkable. To take another example at random, Joan Baez would not find a secondary world in which violence and killing are good and noble morally possible. In other words, each of us has certain expectations about how bad (or good) things could be, and any secondary world we create will be influenced by these expectations.

Now a Christian will not necessarily create a Christian secondary world — Tolkien did not. (Although perhaps a theist may be unable to conceive of a Godless world, because of the nature of theism.) But if he does, what then? Christians will quite possibly find this world one they can enter with special enjoyment (or perhaps not, as we shall see). But for non-Christians, is the Christian nature of such a world a bar to enjoyment? Well, why should it be? A secondary world created by a Buddhist, a Zuñi, a Communist would certainly give us all sorts of insights into

22

Buddhism, the Zuñi religion and outlook, or Communism. As Lewis says in *An Experiment in Criticism,*

> The mark of literary reading, as opposed to scientific or other informative reading, is that we need not believe or approve the Logos [the thing said]. Most of us do not believe Dante's universe is at all like the real one. . . . None of us can accept simultaneously Housman's and Chesterton's views of life, or those of Fitzgerald's *Omar* and Kipling. What then is the good of — what is even the defense for — occupying our hearts with stories of what never happened and entering vicariously into feelings which we should try to avoid having in our own person?. . . . The nearest I have got yet to an answer is that we seek an enlargement of our being. We want to be more than ourselves. . . . We want to see with other eyes, to imagine with other imaginations, to feel with other hearts as well as our own." [10]

Elsewhere Lewis says, "I read Lucretius and Dante when (by and large) I agreed with Lucretius, and have read them since I came (by and large) to agree with Dante. I cannot find that this has much altered my experience or at all altered my evaluation of either." [11]

Thus we will find that although Lewis's and Tolkien's fantasies may be read purely as appreciative fantasy, enjoyed simply for their own sake, yet certain views of the world, certain ideas about life, will be discernible in them. It is these views and these ideas that I am especially interested in extracting and analyzing. We will find that such views and ideas often appear in the form of broad "themes" which can be discerned in the fantasies of Lewis and Tolkien.

We have seen in this discussion certain key themes in Tolkien, which we will see echoed in Lewis. They

---

[10] *An Experiment in Criticism* (New York: Cambridge University Press, 1961), pp. 136-37.
[11] Ibid., p. 86.

are, first, that we ought to see the world as a place of wonder and mystery; second, that the modern world seems increasingly to tend to become a place of ugliness and misery; and, finally, that the Christian Story gives us consolation by showing us that the world ends in eucatastrophe. Let us call these The World of Wonder Theme, The Modern Failure Theme, and The Happy Ending Theme.

Both our authors use secondary worlds, yet each uses them in ways of his own and for purposes of his own. But in each of their secondary worlds these three themes can be found, modified by the author's own way of doing things and by the purposes of that particular story.

Let us look first at the sort of secondary world created by each author. Tolkien created — initially in his children's book *The Hobbit* and then in his trilogy *The Lord of the Rings* — a secondary world of imaginary prehistory. It is inhabited by a number of rational species, not only men and other more or less manlike beings such as elves, dwarves, hobbits, ents, orcs or goblins, and trolls, but also beasts which can think and talk, among them dragons and wargs (a sort of wolflike being). There is an alignment of good and evil forces. Some species of beings, such as elves, are wholly on the side of good; some, such as orcs, wholly on the side of evil. But most species are both corruptible and perfectible; individual men, hobbits, and dwarves may be on the side of good or of evil and may change from one side to the other. Some beings are preternaturally good (like Gandalf the wizard), or preternaturally evil (like Sauron in the *Ring* trilogy, and to some degree Smaug in *The Hobbit*); but the focus of attention is never on such beings. The real heroes, and to some extent even the real villains of Tolkien's books, are capable of both good and evil. They stand in danger of corruption like

24

Bilbo and Frodo, or have a chance (which they can accept or reject) of salvation, like Gollum and Saruman.

Nature is generally seen as beneficient. Where particular places (the Misty Mountains, Mirkwood, Mordor) are evil or unfriendly, this is due to the presence, seen or unseen, of evil beings; such places have been good in the past and can be cleansed and restored by the expulsion of the evil beings. Conversely, the presence of good beings, especially elves, can make a region or territory better and more beautiful. Places like Mirkwood, Lothlōrien, the Shire, Mordor have almost the status of characters in their own right. Technology in the sense of architecture or handicraft is good in itself, but subject to corruption. Uncorrupted technology tends to be associated with a golden age in the past, while manifestations of modernity, such as factories, are sinister.

C. S. Lewis created two major secondary worlds, that is his interplanetary trilogy — *Out of the Silent Planet, Perelandra,* and *That Hideous Strength* — and that of his "Chronicles of Narnia," seven stories written for children but enjoyed by many adults. Lewis's secondary worlds are like that of Tolkien in many respects. There are a number of nonhuman, rational species in the trilogy, especially the three Martian species described in *Out of the Silent Planet* and the eldils which appear in all three books. In the Narnia stories there are men, dwarves, giants, and talking beasts of many species as well as a host of evil beings such as hags and werewolves. There is an alignment of good and evil forces in each story, but it is often a different group. Ransom, the hero of *Silent Planet,* is also the hero of *Perelandra,* but in *Strength* he is a remote, demigodlike figure, not unlike Gandalf in the last part of Tolkien's trilogy. The real heroes of *Strength* are perhaps Mark and Jane Studdock, both

25

of whom nearly fail under testing. The child heroes and heroines of the Narnia tales are an overlapping group, with changes from book to book; one of the early heroines has "dropped out" by the end of the series. The villains in both worlds change also, though there is again some overlap. Weston, one of the villains of *Silent Planet*, is the vehicle of demonic forces in *Perelandra*, and Devine, the other villain of the first book, is a minor figure in the gallery of villains in *Strength*. The witch Jadis is the villainess of two of the Chronicles of Narnia, another witch the villainess of another, and evil men and beasts are the villains of others. There are preternaturally good and evil beings: good and evil eldils in the space trilogy, and in the Narnia stories, Aslan on the one hand and the witches and their allies on the other. But, as with Tolkien, the real focus is on the corruptible or perfectible characters.

As in Tolkien, nature is almost a character in the drama: Malacandra (Mars) and Perelandra (Venus) are parts of the stories set on them, not mere backgrounds. In *Strength* a mythical Arthurian Britain gives a "depth" to the English setting. The land of Narnia and its neighboring kingdoms are similarly important in the Chronicles. Although Lewis's supposed antiscientific attitude has been exaggerated by critics, there is some tendency in his books to idealize the bucolic and primitive and to show the dangers of science and technology. Because of the nature of the secondary worlds in question, there is more of this in the space trilogy than in Tolkien and less of it in the Chronicles of Narnia.

These brief descriptions suggest two themes which should be added to our previous list. The first, which we will call The Good vs. Evil Theme, is that the world is in a state of conflict between good and evil. The second, a corollary of this, is that each of us can and must choose his side in this conflict. We will call this The Choice Theme.

It may now be clear how Tolkien and Lewis embody the first three themes we listed in their secondary worlds. The World of Wonder Theme is introduced indirectly by describing secondary worlds in such a way that we return to contemplate the primary world with new eyes. The Modern Failure Theme is introduced by isolating certain undesirable features of the modern world and showing them in contrast with other values. In contrast to the greenness of the Shire, for example, Mordor's blackness is more apparent, and we realize with a shock that the modern world is closer to Mordor than to the Shire. Associating ugliness and misery with moral evil has some dangers, which we shall examine; but it is an association which Tolkien and Lewis believed in and could argue for. Thus the combination of these elements in the secondary worlds begs no questions which they are not prepared to answer elsewhere.

The Happy Ending Theme is embodied by our authors in their secondary worlds in two ways. Lewis confronts it most directly in the Chronicles of Narnia, which contain events parallel (though not always in an obvious fashion) to the creation of the world, the death and resurrection of Christ, and the final judgment. The space trilogy contains an averted fall of man in *Perelandra* and an apocalyptic ending in *Strength*. Tolkien — who found the Narnia stories, at least, "too allegorical" — attacks this theme in a much more indirect way. However, as we shall see, he manages to give a new expression to one of the most difficult yet most important ideas in Christianity, the idea of vicarious atonement.

The Good vs. Evil Theme is obviously present in the *Lord of the Rings*, to such an extent that novelist critic Edmund Wilson accused Tolkien of having an oversimplified "black and white" picture of morality. [12] Most of the Narnia books and all of the space trilogy similarly describe battles between good and evil forces. Perhaps the books in which the struggle is the least clear are *The Hobbit*, where the original motives of the "good guys" are somewhat mixed, and *The Voyage of the Dawn Treader*, one of the most delightful of the Narnia series but the most episodic. (There is not one clear-cut confrontation between good and evil, but a number of tests of courage and moral stamina.) Yet, even with these exceptions, all the books we have been discussing could be described as stories of a conflict between good and evil forces.

The Choice Theme is presented in a variety of ways by Lewis and Tolkien, sometimes explicitly, as for example in some of the things which Gandalf says to Frodo. Sometimes this is implicit, as in the moral struggles that go on in the heroes and in the subsidiary characters. Indeed, this moral struggle is, in a way, the main focus of much of the story. When Ransom in the space trilogy and Frodo in *The Lord of the Rings* are to some degree lifted above the moral struggle, the focus of the stories shifts away from them to other characters.

Let us consider the Lewis-Tolkien view in relation to its "anti-view," the view which consists of the opposites of the five themes we have been discussing. We can state these roughly as follows. The world is pointless and absurd, and therefore, like all pointless and absurd things, ultimately dull and boring. The modern world with its physical comfort and technological marvels is as near to paradise as we are likely to come; the urgent problem is to extend this "high standard of living" to as many people as possible and

---

12 "Oo Those Awful Orcs." *Nation*, 14 April 1956.

make it last as long as possible. Far from having a happy ending, the world will ultimately end "not with a bang but a whimper," and no matter how great the triumphs of the human race, that race will ultimately die. The universe will outlast us, but our story will inevitably end in futility. "Good" and "evil" are purely emotional reactions to the universe; they have no ground in the nature of the universe and are at best the shibboleths of our tribe or nation. There is no great moral drama in which the individual has a part: at best our moral choices can make life somewhat more livable for ourselves and those close to us. Such a view is in many respects the characteristic "modern" view of the universe. Not all who call themselves modern would share it in all respects, but they would recognize that in challenging any of its tenets they are challenging the prevailing orthodoxy.

The strong person, facing such a view of the universe, may find consolation in work or in personal relationships, or in working to give others what happiness he can. Even he may sometimes falter and find a certain hollowness in triumphs doomed to eventual futility. The weaker person will turn to drugs or submerge himself in sex or violence, pulling the covers over his head to hide the bleak picture. But he, too, is ultimately unsuccessful. Hiding under the covers doesn't remove the bogey, if real, or the fear of the false bogey. If this is the way things are, then we must face the knowledge as best we can. But the good news from Narnia and Middle-earth is that the modern view is false in whole and in part. The story that is told is "Fear not, I have overcome the world." And to those who have drunk the bitterness of the modern view, "There is no tale told which we would rather find is true."

To return to the question which opened the chapter, "Why Fantasy?" we can now see that there are three answers to this question. First, "fantasy remains a human right"; the mind demands "vacations" as well as the body, and after our mental holiday we may return to our tasks in the world refreshed, renewed, and with a new vision. But second, appreciative fantasy, just because it makes no direct statement about the world, paradoxically is the best way to see the beauty and danger of the real world. By recovering the vision and appreciation that fantasy gives us, we learn to see again the world as it is. And finally, it is the consolation of fantasy, the echo in our hearts of the greatest Happy Ending, which makes the fantasy of Lewis and Tolkien so valuable to so many of us. Escape, Recovery, Consolation: these are answers enough, and more than enough, to the question, "Why Fantasy?"

chapter 2

Fantasy and Literature

Even though we can now see that fantasy serves important purposes — Escape, Recovery, Consolation — we may still wonder about the *literary* value of the fantasies of Lewis and Tolkien. Are these fantasies to be considered as literature, or are they subliterary or at least nonliterary? The difficulty in answering these questions is that there are many theories as to what gives a work literary value. Those who are quick to condemn works they dislike as "not literature" are not always equally ready to give a clear and coherent theory of what is and what is not literature.

In his capacity as a professor of English literature, Lewis himself gave a clear and interesting account of how to distinguish literature from nonliterary works. Lewis's theory, as expressed in his book *An Experiment in Criticism*, runs contrary to much that has recently been thought and said about literature. However, like all of Lewis's writing, the book is vigorous and provocative; even those who do not agree with Lewis will find his views a stimulus to think out their own views more clearly. Let us first look at the essentials of Lewis's theory and then see how it applies to his own work and that of Tolkien.

31

The "experiment" spoken of in the book's title is a reversal of the usual process, in which we judge the worth of a book by some set of criteria and then judge readers by the sort of books they enjoy. Lewis suggests that, instead, we look at different sorts of readers and the sort of reading they do and judge books by the sort of reading they receive. "Let us try to discover," Lewis says, "how far it might be plausible to define a good book as a book which is read in one way, and a bad book as a book which is read in another." [1] Lewis points out that the "nonliterary," whom he is careful to distinguish from the uneducated or the vulgar, reads books in quite a different way from the "literary" reader.

On the most obvious level the nonliterary reader (who, remember, might be a great saint, a great scientist, or a great statesman) never reads anything twice, turns to reading only as a last resource, and does not seem to be greatly affected by any literary experience. A more important contrast between the literary "few" and the nonliterary "many," however, is that

> as a result of their different behavior in reading, what they have read is constantly and prominently present to the mind of the few, but not to that of the many. The former mouth over their favorite lines and stanzas in solitude. Scenes and characters from books provide them with a sort of iconography by which they interpret or sum up their own experience. They talk to one another about books often and at length. The latter seldom think or talk about their reading. . . . It is pretty clear that the majority, if they spoke without passion and were fully articulate, would not accuse us of liking the wrong books, but of making such a fuss about any books at all. [2]

[1] *An Experiment in Criticism* (New York: Cambridge University Press, 1961), p. 1.
[2] Ibid., pp. 2-3.

A further analysis of the reading of the nonliterary discloses some less obvious characteristics, which may be summed up as a preference for pure narrative and a disregard for rhythm, style, description, character, and the like. In fact, Lewis says, "they enjoy narratives in which the verbal element is reduced to the minimum — 'strip' stories told in pictures, or films with the least possible dialogue." The unliterary reader "ignores nearly all that the words before him are doing; he wants to know what happens next" (p. 30). It is important to emphasize that Lewis does not mean to deprecate the narrative element in literature — he elsewhere defends it strongly. In *Experiment* Lewis says, "Let us be quite clear that the unliterary are unliterary not because they enjoy stories in these ways, but because they enjoy them in no other. Not what they have but what they lack cuts them off from the fullness of literary experience."[3]

In exploring the proper place of narrative in literature, Lewis makes a digression — highly relevant for our purposes — on myth and fantasy. Myth he describes as

a particular kind of story which has a value in itself — a value independent of its embodiment in any literary work. . . . The pleasure of myth depends hardly at all on such usual narrative attractions as suspense or surprise. . . . Human sympathy is at a minimum . . . the experience may be sad or joyful, but is always grave . . . [and] not only grave but awe inspiring. We feel it to be numinous. It is as if something of great moment had been communicated to us."[4]

In addition, "myth is always in one sense of that word 'fantastic.' It deals with impossibles and preternaturals." This leads Lewis to a discussion of fantasy.

---

3 Ibid., p. 38.
4 Ibid., p. 44.

33

He distinguishes the literary and psychological senses of fantasy: "As a literary form of fantasy means almost any narrative that deals with impossibles and preternaturals." In the psychological sense, Lewis identifies fantasy as "an imaginative construction which in some way pleases." Where such a construction is mistaken for reality, it becomes delusion; where it is "entertained incessantly and to his injury" by the subject, Lewis calls it Morbid Castle-Building; and where it is "indulged in moderately and briefly as a temporary holiday or recreation, duly subordinated to more effective and outgoing activities," Lewis calls it Normal Castle-Building (pp. 50-52).

This Normal Castle-Building may be Egoistic or Disinterested. If egoistic, the daydreamer is the hero of the story and derives satisfaction from imaginary triumphs. If disinterested, the daydreamer merely amuses himself by stories or pictures. "There is thus, if the day-dreamer has any talent, an easy transition from disinterested castle-building to literary invention." [5] Lewis notes that the unliterary reader often uses fiction for the purposes of egoistic castle-building, identifying himself with a book's heroic or fortunate characters. Thus the unliterary reader does not like literary fantasy.

> Though they do not mistake their castle-building for reality, they want to feel that it might be. . . . A story which introduces the marvellous, the fantastic says by implication 'I am merely a work of art. You must take me as such.' . . . The more completely a man's reading is a form of egoistic castle-building the more he will demand a certain superficial realism, and the less he will like the fantastic. [6]

The mention of realism leads to a distinction between realism of presentation and realism of content.

[5] Ibid., p. 53.
[6] Ibid., p. 56.

A fantasy may have great realism of presentation: "the dragon sniffling along the stone in Beowulf . . . the pinnacles in Gawain that looked as if they were 'pared out of paper' . . . the fairy bakers in Huon rubbing the paste off their fingers. . . ."[7] In fact,

the two realisms are quite independent. You can get that of presentation without that of content, as in medieval romance; or that of content without that of presentation as in French (and some Greek) tragedy; or both together as in War and Peace; or neither as in the Furioso or Rasselas or Candide. In this age it is important to remind ourselves that all four ways of writing are good and masterpieces can be produced in any of them.[8]

Lewis points out that many examples of great literature (The Iliad, Oedipus Rex, Hamlet, The Miller's Tale) are not "true to life" in the sense of telling about the sort of thing which normally or expectably happens. "Even if the stories permit the conclusion 'Life is such that this is possible' can anyone believe that they invite it? . . . They are not, in any sense that matters, representations of life as we know it, and were never valued for being so."[9] Literary fantasy does not "give a false picture of life" in the sense of deceiving the reader. "The real danger lurks in sober-faced novels where all appears to be very probable, but all is in fact contrived to put across some social or ethical or religious or anti-religious 'comment on life'"[10]

Having noted some parts of Lewis's theory important for my purposes, I can more briefly describe his conclusions. Lewis shows that on his theory "the ideally bad book is one of which a good reading is impossible. The words in which it exists will not bear

[7] Ibid., p. 58.
[8] Ibid., pp. 59-60.
[9] Ibid., pp. 64, 66.
[10] Ibid., p. 68.

close attention, and what they communicate offers you nothing unless you are prepared either for mere thrills or for flattering day dreams." [11] The good book, on the other hand, permits, invites, and ideally *compels* good reading. "We start from the assumption that whatever has been found good by those who really and truly read probably is good." [12]

How does Lewis's theory apply to his own works and Tolkien's? I would argue that the readers of these works read them in a way that marks them as "literary" rather than "nonliterary" readers; that none of these works as a whole is a "myth" in Lewis's sense, although portions of them have the qualities Lewis ascribes to myth; [13] and that though these works lack realism of content, in very different ways they make use of realism of presentation to achieve their ends. I would also claim that on Lewis's theory, his own and Tolkien's imaginative works are very good books indeed, and Lewis's theory, though not without faults, has considerable advantages over any rival theory.

To begin with the weakest and most indirect evidence that Lewis's and Tolkien's works are "literary," a major portion of the sale of Tolkien's *Ring* trilogy and Lewis's space trilogy is in college bookstores, and a great number of college students and faculty members seem to have read and enjoyed one or both. But this, it might be argued, is true also of *Playboy*. More important is the evidence from various sources that many who have read either Tolkien's or Lewis's fictional works return to them for frequent rereadings and find in them a reading experience of great im-

---

[11] Ibid., pp. 113-14.
[12] Ibid., p. 112.
[13] These works are, of course, fantasies in the literary sense of fantasy, but do not characteristically inspire delusion, morbid castle-building or egoistic castle-building, for reasons which are clear enough from Lewis's discussion.

portance. As Peter Beagle, a brilliant young novelist and observer of the American scene, [14] writes in an introduction to a collection of Tolkien's shorter pieces,

The Lord of the Rings and its prologue, The Hobbit, belong, in my experience, to a small group of books and poems and songs that I have truly shared with other people. The strangest strangers turn out to know it, and we talk about Gandalf and mad Gollum and the bridge of Khazad-dûm while the party or the classroom or the train rattles along unheard. Old friends rediscover it, as I do — to browse through any book of the Ring trilogy is to get hooked once more into the whole legend — and we talk of it at once as though we had just read it for the first time, and as though we were remembering something that had happened to us together long ago. Something of ourselves has gone into reading it, and so it belongs to us. [15]

Stella Gibbons, a novelist perhaps best known for her wickedly delightful satire Cold Comfort Farm, says of Lewis's imaginative writing that science fiction

in the right hands . . . can appear what she truly is: Poetry's younger sister. Lewis had those right hands. His three novels of science fiction . . . hold all that we ask of this kind of story and they are also poetry; of a very old, pure, and satisfying kind, and packed with allegory and myth. . . .

Lewis as a writer of imaginative fiction had superb authority. . . . what can be more astonishing than to imagine the soil and scents and noises on a speck of fire millions of miles from the Earth so vividly that

[14] To substantiate the first claim, look at his novels, *A Fine and Private Place* and *The Last Unicorn.* For the second, see his *I See By My Outfit.* All are published by Ballantine Books, New York.

[15] Peter Beagle, "Tolkien's Magic Ring," an introduction to *The Tolkien Reader* (New York: Ballantine Books, 1966), p. x. The piece originally appeared in *Holiday* magazine, © 1966.

the reader can actually feel a nostalgia for them, as if they had been personally experienced? But even more marvelous are Lewis's accounts of the creatures that live on Malacandra. In their creation, his gift soars until it touches the fringes of that region in Shakespeare's nature out of which the poet drew Ariel and Caliban. [16]

It would be easy enough to multiply such testimony, but it is also easy enough to prove to yourself that Lewis's and Tolkien's books permit and invite good reading.

Perhaps surprisingly, none of the works as a whole is a myth in Lewis's sense. Beagle describes Tolkien's book as embodying "a legend." Miss Gibbons describes Lewis's books as "packed with allegory and myth." But it is fairly obvious that neither set of stories is "extraliterary" in the sense that its plot has a value which is completely independent of its embodiment. Other criteria of Lewis are not satisfied: neither human sympathy nor the comic element is lacking. I think, however, that we are tempted to use such words as "myth" or "legend" (both in their dictionary sense appropriate only to "a traditional story of unknown authorship . . . handed down for generations"), because both Lewis's stories and Tolkien's satisfy the last criterion Lewis lists for myth: "We feel it to be numinous. It is as if something of great moment had been communicated to us." We may note, however, that myths in Lewis's sense may be part of the total machinery of a Lewis or Tolkien story. In discussing myth Lewis gives among his examples the conception of the ents and of Lothlōrien from the Rings trilogy. Similar mythical substructures could easily be found in Lewis's books.

---

[16] Stella Gibbons, "Imaginative Writing," in *Light on C. S. Lewis*, ed. Jocelyn Gibb et al. (New York: Harcourt, Brace & World, 1965), pp. 87, 89.

Tolkien and Lewis use, in different ways, realism of presentation. This is obvious enough in Lewis's case. His vivid descriptions of extraterrestrial scenes and nonhuman entities, the acute observation of character, the realism of the dialogue, all make it easy to suspend disbelief. Stella Gibbons notes with delight, "How skillfully he introduced what may be called the 'stiffening' into these tales, the introduction of *invented fact* — in some cases of actual fact — to give credibility to the incredible!" [17]

One amusing instance of this is the way in which Ransom, the imaginary hero of *Silent Planet*, is linked to the real Lewis, who appears as a minor character in the last chapter of the story. Lewis supposedly writes to Ransom, a philologist, and asks him about the word *Oyarses* which occurs in the twelfth century Platonist Bernardus Silvestris: "I asked C. J. about it and he says it ought to be *Ousiarches*. That of course would make sense, but I do not feel quite satisfied. Have you by any chance ever come across a word like *Oyarses*?" Ransom has, in the story: it is the title of the tutelary spirit or "Intelligence" of the planet Malacandra (Mars). [18] Now look at Lewis's perfectly serious and scholarly work, *The Allegory of Love*, which made his reputation as a scholar of medieval and Renaissance literature.

> In Bernardus Sylvestris, on reaching the *aplanon* or sphere of the fixed stars, we have the following:
>
> Illic Oyarses quidem erat at genius. . . .
>
> The name *Oyarses*, as Professor C. C. J. Webb has pointed out to me, must be a corruption of ουσιαρχης; and he has kindly drawn my attention to Pseudo-

---

[17] Ibid., p. 88.
[18] *Out of the Silent Planet* (New York: The Macmillan Co., 1965), p. 58.

39

Apuleius Asclepius (xix), where the ousiarch of the fixed stars . . . [19]

This is almost art for art's sake — not one out of a hundred of the readers of *Silent Planet* would be likely to know that passage from *Allegory*. But it helps the air of authenticity which Lewis created so well that people often wrote him to ask if *Silent Planet* was a true story. This was part of the same element in Lewis's character which made him translate passages from Latin authors into sixteenth century English, since "when passages from Calvin, Scalinger or Erasmus in modern English jostle passages from vernacular authors with all the flavour of their period about them, it is fatally easy to get the feeling that the Latinists are somehow more enlightened, less remote, less limited by their age than those who wrote English." [20] How few authors, other than Lewis, could have seen the danger, remedied it so brilliantly, or have thought to apologize that he had not done the translation to sixteenth century English "simply for the fun of it"!

With Tolkien we get apparently a rather different situation. One criticism made of Tolkien is that his language is general, unspecific, not evocative of particular images unlike that of D. H. Lawrence, for example. [21] But Tolkien writes in this way on theory and of set purpose. As some scattered remarks make clear, Tolkien distrusts overspecific description in fantasy for the same reason he is wary of pictures in such books: both have the effect of dragooning the

[19] *The Allegory of Love* (New York: Oxford University Press, 1925), p. 362.

[20] *English Literature in the Sixteenth Century Excluding Drama* (New York: Oxford University Press, 1954), preface.

[21] Cf. Burton Raffell, "The Lord of the Rings as Literature," in *Tolkien and the Critics,* ed. Neil D. Isaacs and Rose A. Zimbardo (Notre Dame, Ind.: University of Notre Dame Press, 1968).

imagination, forcing us to see the scene in a certain way.

> However good in themselves, illustrations do little good to fairy-stories. The radical distinction between all art (including drama) that offers a *visible* presentation and true literature is that it imposes one visible form. Literature works from mind to mind and is thus more progenitive. It is at once more universal and more poignantly particular. If it speaks of *bread* or *wine* or *stone* or *tree*, it appeals to the whole of these things, to their ideas; yet each hearer will give to them a peculiar personal embodiment in his imagination. Should the story say "he ate bread," the dramatic producer or painter can only show "a piece of bread" according to his taste or fancy, but the hearer of the story will think of bread in general and picture it in some form of his own. If a story says "he climbed a hill and saw a river in the valley below," the illustrator may catch, or nearly catch, his own vision of such a scene; but every hearer of the words will have his own picture, and it will be made out of all the hills and rivers and dales he has ever seen, but specially out of The Hill, The River, The Valley which were for him the first embodiment of the word. [22]

On this view Tolkien understandably avoids specificity of description. In this rather compressed discussion (it occurs in a note to the essay) Tolkien perhaps exaggerates the difference between pictorial art and literature in general. But certainly the generality of his descriptions is intentional, at worst the result of a mistaken theory, not of a failure to realize a need or satisfy a felt need. Incidentally, his critic gives an unintentional example of the pitfalls of over-specificity; the critic's example of vivid description is "shiny new Grand Rapids furniture." In an informal

---

[22] "Tree and Leaf" in *The Tolkien Reader* (New York: Ballantine Books, 1966), p. 80.

poll of my students, none knew what Grand Rapids furniture was or might be like!

Tolkien, like Lewis, provides "stiffening" to his fantasy by linking it with his own scholarly interests — the study of ancient manuscripts and ancient languages. In the appendices to *The Lord of the Rings* Tolkien provides an elaborate background to the main story: its supposed sources in such imaginary manuscripts as the Red Book of Westmarch, the full story of legends and histories which are alluded to in the story, and a discussion of the languages, names, and alphabets used in the story. Part of the story's delight, whether we read the appendices or not, is the careful work which has gone into this background. Imitators of Tolkien merely give us a mosaic of strange names and strange stories, drawn from various sources, which do not "hang together" in the way in which Tolkien's names do. An elvish name in Tolkien is perspicuously elvish, a dwarvish name noticeably unlike elvish names and like other dwarvish ones. Tolkien's characters always speak and act in character; not only personally (Gandalf always acts Gandalf-like) but, so to speak, *racially* (Legolas and Galadriel are both in their own way elvish). The customs, legends, and histories of the Rohirrim are of a piece with each other and with their names. (Tolkien helps himself here by drawing some of the Rohan material from real Anglo-Saxon words and customs.) Some of us enjoy "going behind the scenes" and seeing the careful work which gives us this sense of authenticity. But all who enjoy Tolkien are enjoying in part the fruits of this meticulous preparation. Tolkien's realism of presentation, though unlike Lewis's in some ways, is equally striking.

On Lewis's theory the imaginative works of Tolkien and of Lewis himself come out with very high marks, and that is clear enough; certainly they are read in the "literary" way by many readers and have values far beyond those of simple narrative. But, one might cynically claim, the theory may have been designed for just that purpose and have no real support. On the theory, the books are good, but is the theory good? Lewis's thesis in *Experiment* is essentially that any book which allows and invites good reading is a good book. Many people would admit the converse of this, that any book allows and invites good reading. It would seem hard to defend the contradictory, that some good books neither allow nor invite good reading. But some people might want to claim that some books which allow and invite good reading are not good books.

Let us see how this may be done. We must reject at the outset any confusion of the contradictory of Lewis's thesis with the mere assertion that some books which are read with enjoyment are not good books. Lewis's discussion explicitly allows for this — a book may be enjoyed because it satisfies a desire for egoistic castle-building, or a desire for mere thrills, and so on. But such motives for enjoyment will not satisfy the criteria Lewis has set down for good reading. For example, those who read merely for thrills will not reread, and those who read for egoistic castle-building will not choose fantasy.

Any theory, however, which denied any connection between enjoyment and literature would thereby reduce itself to absurdity. So it must be that any viable criticism of Lewis's theory would have to show that there are enjoyable experiences of reading — not reducible to ego satisfaction or thrill-seeking and therefore superficially like "genuine" literary experience — which fail some important test of genuineness. Notice that such a criticism cannot deny the enjoyment or reduce it to the *obviously* nonliterary (thrill-seeking, etc.) without conflicting with fact. Thus, such a criticism is not like the accusation that Jack is not attracted to Jill at all, or the accusation that he merely lusts after her. It is, rather, like the accusation that he does not *really* love her. (Perhaps he is merely "in love with love" or is in love with an imaginary person of his own creation.)

It seems to me there are several grounds on which critics have argued that the works of Lewis and Tolkien give merely "pseudoliterary" enjoyment and that these would cover most of the plausible grounds for calling enjoyment of a book "pseudoliterary." It might be alleged that one's enjoyment of a book was pseudo-literary (1) because of banality, (2) because of propaganda, or (3) because while purporting to satisfy literary needs it is, in fact, valued for satisfying psychological or emotional needs (e.g., for reassurance). We will consider these accusations in turn.

1. The accusation of banality. The word "banal" neatly wraps up a series of accusations made against Tolkien and Lewis by their critics. "Banal" can mean "trite," "hackneyed," or "commonplace" or "trivial." Furthermore, the accusation of banality may refer to either language or ideas. The basic assumption behind the accusation of banality seems to be that new ways of expression and new ideas are always to be preferred to old. Now "this is newer than that, therefore this is superior to that" is, as it stands, a plain non sequitur. With regard to language, presumably the bridge between "this is newer" and "this is better" is the supposed principle that new ways of expression invariably do a better job of conveying ideas, impressions, and emotions. But this principle seems to be merely false. Aside from the difficulties it leads to in dealing with much recognized great literature (e.g., the use of stock epithets in Homer), the principle seems to be simply an expression of naive, chronological provincialism: "You must not make people in your book talk that way because this is not the way people talk now."

An allied accusation is that the language in, for example, the *Rings* is "derivative," full of echoes of other literature. This general type of accusation was elegantly put by Samuel Johnson. Boswell questioned him about some poems.

> Boswell: Is there not imagination in them, Sir?
> Johnson: Why Sir, there is in them what *was* imagination, but it is no more imagination in *him* than sound is sound in the echo. And his diction too is not his own. We have long ago seen *white-robed innocence* and *flower-bespangled meads*. [23]

Of course, this is a highly relative matter. If you have not read the other literature you will miss the echoes, and if you read *The Hobbit* before *Beowulf*, the dragon in *Beowulf* is likely to remind you of Smaug rather than vice versa. But again there is a principle behind the accusation, the principle that originality is valuable in itself and lack of originality vitiates any other merits a work may have. Yet, prevalent as this assumption is, it seems also to be false. Originality in itself does not make a work good, for a work can be a failure in an entirely new way. Complete originality is impossible; any work has a great deal in common with works that have gone before. Furthermore, originality is a matter of degree; a completely unoriginal work would have to be an exact copy of another work. Traditional material traditionally treated occurs in many admittedly great works of literature. The idea that interesting work can no longer be done in some traditional form is always open to refutation by counter-example.

But there is also a confusion here between two kinds of unoriginality. Tolkien is unoriginal in his images in one way, original in another. He is unoriginal in that he uses familiar associations — light

---

[23] *Boswell's Life of Johnson*, Tuesday 5 July 1763.

with goodness, darkness with evil, for example. And as Lewis says in *The Allegory of Love*:

It is of the very nature of thought and language to represent what is immaterial in picturable terms. What is good or happy has always been high like the heavens and bright like the sun. Evil and misery were deep and dark from the first. Pain is black in Homer and goodness is a middle point for Alfred no less than for Aristotle. To ask how these married pairs of sensibles and insensibles first came together would be a great folly; the real question is how they ever came apart. [24]

However, the use Tolkien makes of these familiar images is far from unoriginal. Lewis, in *A Preface to Paradise Lost*, makes a similar point about Milton.

There is, furthermore, a special reason why mythical poetry ought not to attempt novelty in respect of its ingredients. What it does with the ingredients may be as novel as you please. But giants, dragons, paradises, gods, and the like are themselves the expression of certain basic elements in man's spiritual experience. In that sense they are more like words — the words of a language which speaks the else unspeakable — than they are like the people and places in a novel. To give them radically new characters is not so much original as ungrammatical. . . . The whole art consists not in evoking the unexpected, but in evoking with a perfection and accuracy beyond expectation the very image that has haunted us all our lives. The marvel about Milton's Paradise or Milton's Hell is simply that they are there — that the thing has at last been done — that our dream stands before us and does not melt. Not many poets can thus draw out leviathan with a hook. Compared with this the short-lived pleasure of any novelty the poet might have inserted would be a mere kickshaw. [25]

[24] *Allegory*, p. 44.
[25] *A Preface to Paradise Lost* (New York: Oxford University Press, 1942), pp. 57-58.

Perhaps the strongest accusation that can be made under the head of banality of language may be seen by looking at the dictionary meaning of "trite" — "worn out by constant use, no longer having freshness, originality or novelty; hackneyed, stale." But certainly such an accusation completely fails to apply to Tolkien or Lewis; far from being worn out by *constant* use, the "high style" sometimes used by Tolkien and Lewis is almost never seen in other contemporary literature. In Tolkien especially there are parallels to what Lewis, in discussing Milton, describes as

the "grandeur" or "elevation" of the style. . . . this grandeur is produced mainly by three things. (1) The use of slightly unfamiliar words and construction, including archaisms. (2) The use of proper names, not solely nor chiefly for their sound, but because they are the names of splendid, remote, terrible, voluptuous, or celebrated things. They are there to encourage a sweep of the reader's eye over the richness and variety of the world — to supply that *largior aether* which we breathe as long as the poem lasts. (3) Continued allusion to all the sources of heightened interest in our sense experience (light, darkness, storm, flowers, jewels, sexual love, and the like). [26]

Archaisms, richness, and variety of proper names and imagery taken from sense experiences are all highly characteristic of Tolkien's works.

When we come to supposed banality of ideas, the idea that novelty or originality is the sole criterion is even sillier. Presumably anyone given a choice between truth or originality would choose truth. But both Lewis and Tolkien have been accused of putting forward ideas which are banal in the sense of being commonplace or trivial, on the order of "good is nice and evil is nasty." That this is false can be seen

[26] Ibid., pp. 40-41.

simply by looking at the list of themes in the last chapter. Every one of the themes we found in Tolkien and Lewis, far from being a commonplace, was directly contradicted by the characteristic modern view of the world. And the differences, far from being trivial, went to the root of one's view of life. Furthermore, the view that Tolkien and Lewis utter mere trivial commonplaces in completely contradictory to the next accusation — propagandizing — though it is often made by the same critics. Let us, then, examine this second charge.

2. The accusation of propaganda. The accusation that the works of Tolkien, or more especially those of Lewis, are vitiated by propagandistic aims can hardly be the accusation that they contain a characteristic view of life or that they take a position for or against certain things. For if this prevented a work from being literature, many admittedly great works of literature (Lucretius, Dante, and Dostoyevsky, for example) would be disqualified. The accusation, then, must be that the propaganda is so overdone that it detracts from the literary value of the work and can be applauded only by partisans of a cause. This accusation is at least partly refuted by the fact that Lewis and Tolkien are admired by intelligent readers and critics who are entirely out of sympathy with their basic assumptions and ideas. Since Tolkien is less explicit than Lewis about some of his deep convictions, critics sometimes attempt to interpret him as "really" sympathetic in whole or in part to their views. This is much harder to do with Lewis, but many readers totally out of sympathy with his ideas have nevertheless admired him. [27]

---

[27] See, for example, Gilbert Highet's "From World to World" in *People Places and Books* (New York: Oxford University Press, 1953).

In fact, the accusation of propaganda seems to come most often from those violently opposed to Lewis's and Tolkien's basic conviction and afraid of their apparent success in making them attractive to others. It is thus not really a literary criticism at all but a philosophical one: "These ideas are false and you do a disservice by propagating them." But philosophical criticism must be backed by argument, and those who accuse Lewis and Tolkien of propaganda are notably short of arguments for their view. Indeed, their main techniques seem to be direct and indirect sneers and more or less flat assertions that certain ideas cannot be believed. [28] Such devices are unlikely to persuade any person not already persuaded, and even he may feel some embarrassment if this is the best his champion can do.

3. The accusation of wish-fulfillment. This is a curious accusation, for presumably hardly anyone gives primary belief to Tolkien's Middle-earth or its inhabitants, and those who believe in explicitly Christian ideas which occur in Lewis have ground for their belief outside of Lewis's fictional works. Those who seek reassurance will surely look for it in new or established religions or philosophies, which make a claim to primary belief, and not in explicitly fictional works, which lay claim only to secondary belief. Of course, any vividly imagined work may produce primary belief in the unsophisticated or unstable, but this is as true of Homer as of Tolkien, or as true of Dante as of Lewis.

---

[28] Some notable practitioners of these techniques are Catherine Stimpson, *J. R. R. Tolkien* (New York: Columbia University Press, 1969); William Ready, *Understanding Tolkien and the Lord of the Rings* (New York: Paperback Library, 1969), orig. title: *The Tolkien Relation*; and Mary Ellman, "Growing Up Hobbitic," in *New American Review*, no. 2, New American Library, 1968. Their main target is Tolkien, but there are oblique attacks on Lewis, especially in Ready.

I think these sorts of accusations do point to some weak places in Lewis's theory, some possibilities he has not considered. Someone may read a book in the "literary" way, yet it may be true that the book he enjoys is a mere imitation of better works with which he is unfamiliar. Someone may misunderstand his delight in seeing agreeable views well expressed, or his pleasure in wish-thinking for literary enjoyment. But these holes in Lewis's theory are easily plugged, and when they are, the theory is left stronger than before. The approach of judging books by the kind of reading they admit and invite seems more and more attractive as we probe and test it.

And after all, what alternative is there to Lewis's theory? Even if we were ready to hand over our judgment of literature to experts, the experts disagree. If there are clear criteria (different from Lewis's) of literary worth, what are they and who has managed to state and support them? The philosopher, used to clear distinctions and exhaustive argumentation, finds a notable lack of both in most writers about literature. He finds a plethora of confident assertions and a paucity of reasonable backing — except in Lewis.

Of course, to substantiate this point fully would lead us into a complete survey of the present state of aesthetics and the philosophy of literature, which is too much to undertake here. Still, lacking such a survey I fling out at least a challenge: Lewis's theory is clear and well reasoned; it seems to cover the facts on which there is general agreement and to argue persuasively for its distinctive theses. No alternative theory known to me is a serious rival to Lewis's. There may be better theories, but one would have to see the argument.

Finally, as we have seen, both Lewis's and Tolkien's imaginative works come off well by the standards of Lewis's theory. For some readers, at least, if any theory

50

of literature ruled out Lewis's and Tolkien's imaginative works as good books this would in itself be a damaging criticism of that theory. Books are good in different ways, but in their own way the books of Lewis and Tolkien are very good indeed.

chapter 3

Language, Mind, and Character

In any voyage from world to world, language is a problem. If you go to Mars or to Elfland, are the Martians or Elves to speak English or are you to speak their language? If the first, how do you explain the fact to them? And if the second, how do you prevent the learning of the alien language from delaying or obstructing your story? In a children's book you need not face this problem. In Lewis's chronicles the talking beasts of Narnia, the witch Jadis from the dying world of Charn, the Persian-like Calormenes all speak English, apparently (or if not, the English children who are the heroes and heroines of the stories magically understand whatever they do speak). In *The Hobbit* elves, dwarves, trolls, and goblins all speak a language intelligible to each other and to Bilbo the hobbit. But in an adult world this will not do. The "language problem" must be solved.

Lewis and Tolkien solve it, each in characteristic ways. Tolkien supposes a "common speech" spoken by hobbits and men, but constantly uses invented languages with characteristic proper and place names, so that snatches of identifiable elvish or orcish language can be used for literary effect. Lewis makes Ransom's learning of one Martian language an important part of his plot in *Silent Planet* and provides a plausible reason why that language is the Martian *lingua franca* — it is the literary and poetic language, so the scientists and craftsmen, who can express their ideas in any language, learn it. But then, to avoid introducing a new language for Venus, Lewis blandly tells us that the Martian literary language, after all, is a sort of interplanetary *lingua franca*. (The idea of a common language for unfallen creatures may or may not be plausible, but Lewis gives no hint of this when he first talks about the Martian languages.) To defend this device he builds into the story a plot element consisting of a primitive or magical theory of language (that certain sounds are innately suited to certain meanings), which he then uses to good effect in the climax of his story. This is turning one's difficulties into advantages with a vengeance!

To think that Lewis seriously believed in this "magical" theory of language would be a serious mistake, on a par with thinking that he gave primary belief to other plot devices such as the medieval theory of the planets' character and influence or the magical powers of Merlin. No one I know of has made this mistake about Lewis, but an exactly parallel mistake has been made about Tolkien. Because as part of his machinery Tolkien invents a liquid, flowing language for the elves and a harsh dissonant language for the orcs and other villains, he has been accused, with some degree of seriousness, of thinking the letter *l* morally preferable to the letter *k*. [1]

---

[1] Mary Ellman, "Growing Up Hobbitic," in *New American Review,* no. 2, New American Library, 1968, p. 227; Catherine Stimpson, *J. R. R. Tolkien* (New York: Columbia University Press, 1969,, p. 5. Both ignore the fact that dwarvish as well as orcish speech abounds in *k*.

Aside from such devices, however, both Lewis and Tolkien have some serious points to make about language which are well worth examining. For Lewis there is almost an identification of language with rationality. The talking beasts of Narnia — beavers, owls, and mice, for example — are larger than ordinary beasts of the same kind and may even live in houses, use tools, and have political organizations and allegiances. But their real differentia is that they are *talking* beasts. The evil beasts punished by Aslan in the Narnian "last judgment" lose the gift of speech and with it rationality, memory — and immortality!

A more sophisticated version of the same idea occurs in the scene where Ransom meets his first Martian creature.

> The huge seal-like creature seated beside him became unbearably ominous. It seemed friendly; but it was very big, very black, and he knew nothing at all about it. . . . was it really as rational as it appeared?
>
> . . . these sudden losses of confidence . . . arose when the rationality of the *hross* tempted you to think of it as a man. Then it became abominable — a man seven feet high, with a shaky body, covered, face and all, with thick black animal hair, and whiskered like a cat. But starting from the other end you had an animal with everything an animal ought to have — glossy coat, liquid eye, sweet breath and whitest teeth — and added to all these, as though Paradise had never been lost and earliest dreams were true, the charm of speech and reason. [2]

We will return to this identification of speech and rationality in due course, but let us now explore Tolkien's attitude toward language. There are no really talking beasts (in Lewis's sense) in Tolkien if you

---

2 Lewis, *Out of the Silent Planet* (New York: The Macmillan Co., 1965), p. 58.

except Smaug the dragon, a formidable personality and not really a "beast." But each rational species — elf, dwarf, ent, man, and hobbit, orc, and troll — has its own language and its own way of expressing itself. If we say that for Lewis speech is rationality, then for Tolkien speech is personality. The noble speak nobly, the evil speak evilly. This has aroused the derision of some critics, who cannot rid themselves of the modern equation of sincerity with incoherence or the modern belief that there is some virtue in everyone speaking as badly as everyone else. The idea that incoherence is a necessary characteristic of ordinary speech would be equally strange to Irishmen, Iroquois, and Zulus (all nations with a tradition of oratory on great occasions or small), but the idea is prevalent in many modern cultures, especially English-speaking ones. This becomes part of the expectations of many critics when they look for realism of presentation, and not finding this, they ignore the subtler sort of realism which is to be found in Tolkien.

Lewis's departures from pseudonaturalism in this respect are less obvious than Tolkien's, but equally real. What Stella Gibbons says of Lewis could equally be said of Tolkien, "Each being talks as such a being would." This is, of course, unrealistic in the sense that, in "real life," speech is not *always* a revelation of character. But it is such a revelation much more often than most moderns realize.

There is a red herring here that needs to be cleared away. In their children's books, where they are more limited by the form in which they have chosen to write, both Tolkien and Lewis use differences in English style to mark differences in language. Thus, for example, Lewis's Calormenes talk a stately dialect reminiscent of some English translations or imitations of Persian or Arabian authors. Now if Narnia were like our world, the Calormenes would presumably speak a different language than the Narnians; this is what Lewis wants to suggest by his use of the "dialect," at the same time avoiding complications unnecessary in a story of the sort he is writing. For similar reasons Tolkien makes the trolls met by Bilbo in *The Hobbit* speak a sort of cockney dialect. One of his more humorless critics has austerely criticized him for this. "[Bilbo] speaks standard English but [the trolls] speak filthy rough, working-class Cockney. Recently, of course, musical groups have shown us the wit and poetry of working-class English speech." [3] I am afraid that Miss Stimpson meant that last line not as a joke, but as a serious rebuke to Tolkien, and the complex of misunderstandings which it reveals would need a whole chapter to unravel.

Let me try to deal with this misunderstanding as briefly as it deserves. For certain purposes Tolkien has pictured unpleasant characters as talking in a certain way. Presumably, the accusation being made is that by so doing he suggests that all those who talk in this way are unpleasant characters. (The parallel accusation for Lewis would be that all those who say things like "O my father and O the delight of my eyes . . ." are likely to worship monstrous bird-headed gods, which is even more obviously silly.) But the false conversion is the critics' and not Tolkien's. From the relatively limited resources of English dialect, Tolkien has chosen to make the trolls speak rather like Bill Sykes. But it is only the critics who are silly enough to suggest that he means that all those who talk in this way are likely to act like Bill Sykes. (By the way, the real villain of *The Hobbit*, Smaug the dragon, speaks elegant English.)

---

[3] Stimpson, *J. R. R. Tolkien*, p. 13.

The point is perhaps worth pursuing into the more complex relation of speech to character in the adult books. Tolkien describes the orcs as limited in vocabulary and harsh in expression.

> It is said that they had no language of their own, but took what they could of other tongues and perverted it to their own liking; yet they make only brutal jargons, scarcely sufficient for their own needs, unless it were for curses and abuse. And these creatures, being filled with malice, hating even their own kind, quickly developed as many barbarous dialects as there were groups or settlements of their race. [4]

This "invented fact" has the plot advantage that orcs of different groups must converse in Common Speech, so that Merry and Pippin in Book Three, Chapter 11, or Sam in Book Six, Chapter 1, can understand what orcs are saying. It is also connected with the concept of the orcs as purely evil creatures, the "anti-race" of the elves, which we will speak of in Chapter 5. But the more complex and more important villains — Smaug and Saruman, for example — are masters of language (used, of course, for their own evil purposes).

> Suddenly another voice [Saruman's] spoke, low and melodious, its very sound an enchantment. Those who listened unwarily to that voice could seldom report the words that they heard; and if they did they wondered, for little power remained in them. Mostly they remembered only that it was a delight to hear the voice speaking, all that it said seemed wise and reasonable, and desire awoke in them by swift agreement to seem wise themselves. When others spoke they seemed harsh and uncouth by contrast; and if they gainsaid the voice, anger was kindled in the hearts of those under the spell. . . . none were unmoved; none rejected its pleas and its commands

[4] Tolkien, *The Return of the King* (New York: Ballantine Books), p. 511.

without an effort of mind and will so long as its
master had control of it. [5]

Notice that this is a misuse of language to control and
enchant, propaganda to the nth degree. But the simple
equation of those who speak "well" with the heroes
and those who speak "badly" with the villains is obvious, destroyed by the counterexamples of Smaug and
Saruman, so far as Tolkien is concerned. The sense
in which the villains speak "badly" is a purely moral
sense and has distinguished authority: "Out of the ful-
ness of the heart, the mouth speaks."

The clearest example of the same theme in Lewis's
work is the Unman in *Perelandra*. In tempting the
Green Lady, the Unman can use argument and imagery to subtly weave half-truths, and cloudy images.
He speaks "well" in the sense of speaking subtly and
effectively.

> It showed plenty of intelligence when talking to the
> Lady, but Ransom soon perceived that it regarded
> intelligence simply and solely as a weapon, which it
> had no more wish to employ in its off duty hours
> than a soldier has to do bayonet practice when he is
> on leave. Thought was for it a device necessary to
> certain ends, but thought itself did not interest it. [6]

Incidentally, the two passages I have quoted are an
excellent example of Tolkien's and Lewis's contrasted
but equally real masteries of style. Lewis's is more
"modern"; the excellence of the metaphor about bayo-
net practice is the sort of excellence the modern critic
is awake to. But Tolkien's prose casts its own kind of
spell, of which occasional archaisms like "gainsaid" are
a part. Notice the frequent use of words such as

---

[5] Tolkien, *The Two Towers*, rev. ed. (New York: Ballantine
Books, 1969), p. 234.

[6] Lewis, *Perelandra* (New York: The Macmillan Co., n.d.),
p. 128.

"wise," "power," "heart," "enchantment," "spell," which have ancient and complex associations for the reader. Here we find Tolkien making use in practice of something which Lewis has discussed and defended in theory: the use of "stock responses."

For Lewis and Tolkien it is both desirable and legitimate to make use of certain words and ideas which arouse an almost automatic response and to call on a great complex of traditional ideas. For example, to use "the sword of the king" as a metaphor for the power of the state is to make use of certain traditional attitudes and emotions. It is to remind ourselves of Solomon or Arthur, to hear echoes of St. Paul or Christ. The modern tendency is to assume that such responses because they are traditional are bound to be outworn, to have no profound emotional echoes. Tolkien (in much of what he wrote) and Lewis (in some of what he wrote) seem to me to provide a counterexample to this thesis for those with eyes to see. Used badly, the traditional imagery fails; used well it can still stir us. Modern imagery can equally fail; "the clubs and machine guns of the Fascist dictators" as a metaphor for state power regarded unfavorably can become a mere rhetorical cliché, arousing no particular response except boredom.

Lewis, in the first chapter of *The Abolition of Man*, argues that training of our responses to certain ideas (which to a degree means to certain words and phrases) is an indispensable part of a fully human life. Tolkien to some extent presumes responses trained in this way, to some extent offers such a training for those whose hearts are open to it. The "debunking" of Tolkien by certain critics has a great deal in common with the debunking of certain stock responses which Lewis discusses.

But certainly, if stock responses are not to be mere conditioned reflexes imposed on us for certain purposes, they must have some validity. This is the traditional idea, which Lewis defends.

> Until quite modern times all teachers and even all men believed the universe to be such that certain emotional reactions on our part could be either congruous or incongruous to it — believed in fact that objects did not merely receive, but could *merit* our approval or disapproval, our reverence or our contempt. . . . The little human animal will not at first have the right responses. It must be trained to feel pleasure, liking, disgust and hatred at these things which really are pleasant, likeable, disgusting and hateful. . . . Reason in man must rule the mere appetites by means of the "spiritual elements." [7]

Now when Lewis pictures the evil crew at Belbury and contrasts them with Ransom's companions at St. Anne's, or when Tolkien subtly contrasts and compares elves and orcs, the author is using literary means to exaggerate and thereby reinforce certain responses. Malice, treachery, and lying really are detestable, and in Lord Feverstone or Saruman we see them to be so. Friendship, humor, speaking well and living well really are admirable; in Ransom or Elrond we sharpen our appreciation of them. This has caused some to accuse Tolkien and Lewis of "moral didacticism," but it is not, rightly understood, a charge either would reject — though, as Lewis said of Milton, we may sometimes be in "danger of supposing that the poet was inculcating a rule when in fact he was enamoured of a perfection."

One element of the effort to show the admirable as admirable and the detestable as detestable is making the admirable speak admirably and the detestable speak detestably. In their different ways Lewis and Tolkien do this with great success.

---

[7] *The Abolition of Man* (New York: The Macmillan Co., 1961), p. 25.

To return for a moment to the mistaken idea we discussed earlier, it does not follow from this effort that those who speak detestably are detestable. If a man's discourse drips with filthy oaths and shows a poverty of invention and sympathy, it may or may not mark a moral fault. Unfortunate background or early training may remove most of all culpability from him. And a lady who with elegance, invention, and something approaching lyricism backbites, gossips, and denigrates may be morally a hundred times worse, even if the man's language is culpable. Nor is "lower class" language the issue; Sam speaks like a gardener and is a hero, Denetho· speaks like a king and is a villain.

In the last analysis, however, the expectation that character will reveal itself in speech is a not unreasonable one. Speech, while not the only clue to character, is a clue to character. Those who fail to realize this are missing one part of the truth.

The use which Tolkien and Lewis make of language in their fiction grows out of their professional concern with language, in interesting ways. Tolkien's field of specialization is Anglo-Saxon, and some of the things he is known for professionally are an annotated edition of the middle English poem, *Sir Gawain and the Green Knight,* and a perceptive analysis of *Beowulf* and its critics.[8] The study of Anglo-Saxon itself would, I think, have some tendency to influence any imaginative person to think of roots and origins, the means by which language molds and is molded by history. The way in which modern English is built on an Anglo-Saxon foundation with Latin, French, and other

---

[8] *Sir Gawain and the Green Knight,* ed. J. R. R. Tolkien and E. V. Gordon (New York: Oxford University Press, 1925, sec. ed. 1967); "Beowulf: the Monsters and the Critics," most easily available in *An Anthology of Beowulf Criticism,* ed. Lewis E. Nicholson (Notre Dame, Ind.: University of Notre Dame Press, 1963).

borrowings, the way in which an Anglo-Saxon word (*cwik*, for example) can change and evolve over a period of time, has a tendency to remind us of how the present is based on the past and of the great gulf of history which lies behind us. Tolkien's chronologies, histories, and legends in the *Ring* trilogy surely owe something to this habit of mind.

Furthermore, as a philologist, a man professionally concerned with language itself, Tolkien is fascinated by words and their combinations. Some of the more imaginative of us may have made up imaginary worlds, like the land of Boxen which C. S. Lewis and his brother created as children. [9] We may have started with certain characters, created by ourselves or borrowed from literature (my own children took Pooh and Piglet on imaginary adventures through space), and then found ourselves creating a country and a society for them, and finally as an afterthought perhaps some place-names and a few scraps of a language. By his own account, Tolkien's imagination worked the other way, to some extent, in the creation of the *Ring* trilogy. Fascinated by imagined languages, he began to create a world for the languages to be spoken in. This reversal of the usual process is perhaps not fully understandable to those who have not themselves felt the fascination of language or the pleasures of creating a language of one's own.

The middle English poem, *Gawain*, and the Anglo-Saxon epic, *Beowulf*, also probably played their part in influencing Tolkien's imagination. In *Sir Gawain and the Green Knight*, a monstrous green man, riding a green horse, appears at King Arthur's court at Christmas time. The king is delaying his feast until some remarkable incident shall have occurred. The Green

---

[9] See W. H. Lewis's memoir of his brother in *Letters of C. S. Lewis* (New York: Harcourt, Brace & World, 1965).

Knight challenges any one of the knights at the round table to trade blow for blow, using a monstrous axe he carries. The king rashly accepts the challenge, but is forestalled by his nephew Gawain, who takes the wager on his uncle's behalf. Gawain strikes a mighty blow and beheads the Green Knight, but the monster picks up his head and charges Gawain to seek him out in a year and a day to receive the return blow. Gawain has to search out the monster's lair, the Green Chapel, and a few day before he is due to meet the knight he arrives at a nearby castle. The lord of the castle, Bercilac, and his wife entertain Gawain courteously, but Bercilac makes a bargain with Gawain to exchange whatever each gains during Gawain's stay at the castle.

For three days Bercilac goes out to hunt, and Gawain is left at the castle with his wife. The wife attempts to seduce Gawain, who resists her advances and keeps his bargain with her husband by passing on to Bercilac the kisses Gawain has received from his wife. But on the last day the lady tempts Gawain with the gift of a magic green girdle which will prevent him from being killed. Gawain, momentarily putting life before honor, breaks his word to Bercilac by not passing on this "gain." Riding out to meet the Green Knight, Gawain receives three blows from him; the first two are feints but the third wounds Gawain in the neck. The knight reveals himself as Bercilac in enchanted guise and tells Gawain that the two feints were for the two days when Gawain kept his word, the wound for the girdle he failed to pass on according to the terms of the bargain. Bercilac reveals that his appearance at Arthur's court was a plot by Morgan Le Fay to trouble Arthur and Guinevere. He praises Gawain and says that all is quits between them. But Gawain knows he has failed at least partially the test set him, and returns to Arthur's court a sadder but wiser man, bearing the green girdle as a reminder of his failure. When Gawain tells his tale at Arthur's court, however, the whole court assumes green girdles in courtesy and as a mark of respect for Gawain.

It is a strange and fascinating story, even in translation or summary, and the close contact with it that Tolkien had while producing his edition must have had some effect on his imagination. Nothing in the *Ring* trilogy derives directly from it, except possibly Frodo's near-failure at the last moment of his quest, when he refuses to destroy the Ring and is saved only by the last frantic attempt of Gollum to possess it. But the whole atmosphere of wonder and mystery which the anonymous Gawain poet has created reminds one powerfully of Tolkien's writing.

The story of Beowulf is better known. It is essentially the tale of the encounter of Beowulf, the hero, with three monsters: Grendel, Grendel's mother, and the great dragon. The barehanded combat with Grendel, Beowulf's descent into the awful lake to meet the female monster, and the meeting with the fire-drake in his old age each show different aspects of Beowulf's heroism. Tolkien has in fact borrowed an incident from the Beowulf story — the theft of a cup from the dragon's hoard, which is missed by the dragon and sets him off on a rampage that ends with his death at the hands of a hero. But the two incidents are treated quite differently by the Beowulf poet and by Tolkien. A modern translation of Beowulf describes the cup incident as follows:

The ancient scourge that haunts the half-light of dawn . . . [the] smooth-skinned, spiteful dragon seeks out barrows of the dead, and flies by night, burning and encircled in fire; . . . He is wont to seek out what is hoarded in the earth, and there takes up his abode beside the heathen gold, growing wise in ripeness of years, and yet for all that he is no better off. Thus for three hundred years this scourge of the nation guarded that immense house of treasure through his more than human might, until this one man roused fury in his heart. He took the gold-plated flagon to his lord. . . . Thus was the hoard ransacked and the hoarded wealth carried off. . . .

When the serpent awoke . . . he slithered along the rock, and with ruthless rage found the footprints of his foe, for in his stealthy cunning he had stepped too far forward and close to the dragon's head. . . . Eagerly the guardian of the hoard searched along the ground, meaning to find the man who had acted so cruelly towards him as he slept. Burning with savage rage, he went circling again and again round the whole outer wall of the barrow, but there was no one to be found in that waste land. Yet he rejoiced at the thought of a fight and deeds of battle, while from time to time he turned back into the barrow to search for the rich cup; he soon discovered that some man or other had tampered with the gold and the lordly wealth.

The guardian of the hoard . . . sped forth, armed with flame and fire. [10]

Here is Tolkien's view of the parallel incident:

Dragons may not have much real use for all their wealth, but they know it to an ounce as a rule, especially after long possession; and Smaug was no exception. He had passed from an uneasy dream (in which a warrior, altogether insignificant in size but provided with a bitter sword and great courage, figured most unpleasantly) to a doze, and from a doze to wide waking. . . . He stirred and stretched forth his neck to sniff. Then he missed the cup!

Thieves! Fire! Murder! Such a thing had not happened since first he came to the Mountain! His rage

---

[10] *Beowulf and Its Analogues,* tr. G. N. Garmonsway et al. (London: J. M. Dent and Sons Ltd., 1968), pp. 60-61.

passes description — the sort of rage that is only seen when rich folk that have more than they can enjoy suddenly lose something that they have long had but have never before used or wanted. His fire belched forth, the hall smoked, he shook the mountain-roots. . . , and then coiling his length together, roaring like thunder underground, he sped from his deep lair through its great door, out into the huge passages of the mountain-palace and up towards the Front Gate. [11]

Both dragons are fire-breathing monsters who hoard gold and are infuriated at their loss. Yet the dragon in *Beowulf* is like a forest fire or a flood, a sort of natural disaster, while Smaug is a character of some complexity and subtlety.

There is some similarity of atmosphere between parts of *Beowulf* and the *Ring* trilogy. Tolkien's orcs and trolls owe something to Grendel and his mother, and some of the horror of the desolate mere where Grendel's mother dwells has gone into the making of Mirkwood and of the land of Mordor.

But Tolkien has not merely borrowed from the early English epics which he dealt with as a scholar. He has created in our own time a work with something of the same fascination and the same mythical quality. In the making of this story, Tolkien's own experience of language and its history has played its part.

Lewis's professional preoccupation with language took a somewhat different course from Tolkien's. Primarily a scholar of medieval and Renaissance literature, Lewis was especially interested with the way in which words change their meaning and with the misunderstandings which can arise as a result of such change.

---

[11] *The Hobbit* (New York: Ballantine Books, 1969), pp. 207-8.

In his *Studies in Words* Lewis traces the history of a number of important words (such as "nature," "genius," "simple") over a span of hundreds of years and shows how taking such words purely in some familiar modern sense (what Lewis calls the *dangerous sense*) can seriously mislead us in our attempts to understand the writing of an earlier period.

This is a specific application of a more general thesis of Lewis's: the mutual effect of thought on language and language on thought. Take the word "nature" and its equivalents in other languages (e.g., *phusis* in Greek). The word cannot bear its modern sense, as in "let's get out into the woods and enjoy Nature," until Nature can be *contrasted* with something not itself — Nature as opposed to Civilization, Nature (created things) as opposed to God.

But once invented, the concept of Nature can have important effects on our thought.

> Once you can talk about *nature (d.s.)* you can deify it — or "her." Hence the sense which I shall call *Great Mother Nature; nature* used to mean not simply all the things there are, as an aggregate or even a system, but rather some force or mind or *élan* supposed to be immanent in them. It is of course often impossible to be sure in a given instance whether the sense Great Mother Nature implied genuine personalization (a deity believed in) or merely personification as a rhetorical figure. . . .
>
> . . . Even now I am not sure that this meaning is always used purely as a figure, to say what would equally make sense without it. The test is to remove the figure and see how much sense remains. Of all the pantheon Great Mother Nature has, at any rate, been the hardest to kill. [12]

---

[12]Lewis, *Studies in Words* (New York: Cambridge University Press, 1960), pp. 41-42.

One of the more interesting fictional uses Lewis makes of this idea is in the chapter in *Silent Planet* where Ransom is translating for Weston, who is attempting a philosophical justification of his interplanetary imperialism. Weston's grand generalizations about life and evolution when reduced to simple language reveal their emptiness:

As soon as Ransom finished, Weston continued.

"Life is greater than any system of morality; her claims are absolute. It is not by tribal taboos and copy-book maxims that she has pursued her relentless march from the amoeba to man and from man to civilization."

"He says," began Ransom, "that living creatures are stronger than the question whether an act is bent [evil] or good — no, that cannot be right — he says it is better to be alive and bent than to be dead — no — he says, he says — I cannot say what he says, Oyarsa, in your language. But he goes on to say that the only good thing is that there should be very many creatures alive. He says there were many other animals before the first men and the later ones were better than the earlier ones; but he says the animals were not born because of what is said to the young about bent and good action by their elders. And he says these animals did not feel any pity."

"She — " began Weston.

"I'm sorry," interrupted Ransom, "but I've forgotten who She is."

"Life, of course," snapped Weston. [13]

The personification of Life, like the personification of Nature, leads us to say things which in cold prose are ambiguous or nonsensical.

When we look back at the uses of language by our

---

[13] Lewis, *Out of the Silent Planet*, pp. 137-38.

two authors we can see similarities. Both use language to reveal character, both connect language and rationality. But beyond this there are differences — perhaps only differences of emphasis, but important nevertheless. Tolkien uses language to weave enchantments; his use of elvish or orcish words can establish a mood, can create belief in us. Lewis uses language to convince, to enlighten, as well as to make us picture strange scenes and strange beings. Both are poets, both are teachers. But in Tolkien the Poet predominates, in Lewis the Teacher. Both use language to change the way we look at the world, but Tolkien, we might say, works through our emotions, while Lewis works through our intellect. Both use our imaginations; as Lewis says, "In general . . . the poets' route to our emotions lies through our imaginations," and this is true of Tolkien. But there is a route to the intellect through imagination, also, a route utilized both by the satirist and the teller of parables.

It may or may not be true that "a poem should not mean / But be." But this notion provides the grounds for an important distinction between Tolkien and Lewis. Tolkien's Middle-earth is a superbly realized work of the imagination. If we ask "what it means," Tolkien will tell us that a secondary world is valuable in itself; its meaning is its existence. Lewis's *Perelandra* is an equally superb creation, but it is also the setting for a morality play with profound implications. If we ask why it exists, why it was created, this can be explained in terms of a lesson Lewis had to teach: Perelandra's existence is its meaning. The approach to language in the two authors shows something of this dualty, too. For Tolkien, the philologist, language is an end in itself, an object of study, something to enjoy and play with. For Lewis, the professor of literature, language is a tool to be used, a means to express ideas and images. But we must return to the fact that these are differences in emphasis; Lewis wrote *Studies in Words*, Tolkien studied the meaning as well as the language of *Beowulf*. And both writers share a vision of the world in which Existence and Meaning, Being and Wisdom are only different names for one Reality.

Good, Evil,
and God

chapter 4

Good and Evil in Lewis

In one sense neither Lewis nor Tolkien has anything new to say about good and evil — they are both Christians and their morality is traditional Christian morality. Those parts of Christian morality which they have occasion to make use of in their fiction are limited by the nature of those works.

But beyond this there are certain emphasis on parts of Christian morality, certain interpretations of Christian morality in Lewis and Tolkien (not necessarily the same ones in both), which are worth noting. To give a parallel, St. Francis's morality was the basic Catholic moral code, as it was interpreted in his time. But Francis's emphasis on universal charity and voluntary poverty arose from his own vision of what was most important in that code and from his vision of what means could most effectively serve the ends recognized by that code. The parallel is the more interesting in that Francis utilized the enthusiasm for the chivalric ideal, which he shared with many of his contemporaries, to bring to life certain Christian ideals. He spoke, for example, of Poverty as his "Lady" and of himself as her "Troubadour." If the comparison is permissible (and I think it is), this is something like Lewis's utilization of a science-fiction framework and Tolkien's use of fairy-story.

Let me begin with what seems to me to be a fairly basic misunderstanding of Lewis's view of morality. By seeing that it is a misunderstanding we shall gain a better grasp of Lewis's actual view, and by understanding Lewis's interpretation of morality we shall gain some insight into Tolkien.

The misunderstanding occurs in a study of science fiction from a theological perspective, *The Shattered Ring*, by Lois and Stephen Rose. The Roses say Lewis has the "evident purpose" of presenting "a formal 'apology' for a certain body of Christian doctrine,"[1] which seems to me to show an odd idea of what a formal apology for a body of Christian doctrine would be like. But our main concern is with their characterization of Lewis's heroes and villains. About Ransom, the hero of *Silent Planet* and *Perelandra*, they say he "is treated by the author (unconsciously perhaps) as a lovable but rather dumb child" (p. 63). Of the good characters in *Strength* they say, "The good people are all very lovable (if at times a little weak), docile, and always polite" (p. 62). The Roses say Lewis's conception of man is "static" and elsewhere describe his good characters as "passive." Lewis's Malacandrans are described in this way.

> The Martians — clearly meant to embody an old but unfallen world — have no fears of death. But not in [a] fiercely life-affirming manner. . . . On Mars the death-fearlessness stems from resigned submission to the 'true God' Maleldil and to the nature of things; thus their lives are peaceful, unworried, and productive.[2]

---

[1] Lois and Stephen Rose, *The Shattered Ring* (Richmond, Va.: John Knox Press, 1970), p. 60.

[2] Ibid., p. 61.

The consequences of the averted fall on Perelandra are described by the Roses as follows:

> Ransom, the Christian, preserves the natural inno-
> cence of the planet and its two inhabitants, assuring
> that Venus, at least, will not have to reenact the
> tumultuous history of earth, but will drift instead in
> a timeless, conflictless bliss, its inhabitants nestled
> against the benevolent bosom of nature. [3]

The Roses accuse Lewis of thinking that "never to
have fallen is equivalent to redemption" (p. 12) and
later say that "Lewis seems to desire a *return* of man
to the state of instinctive docility which he imagines
Eden to be. But this can hardly be the destiny of
man."

They contrast their understanding of Lewis's view
with Dostoyevsky's "Underground Man," who says,
"Shower upon [man] every earthly blessing. . . . even
then out of sheer ingratitude, sheer spite, man would
play you some nasty trick . . . simply to introduce into
all this positive good sense his fatal fantastic element." [4]

The Roses continue, "Lewis' static conception denies man precisely that element of cantankerous freedom which is the essence of humanity, a freedom
which is more important to man than luxury or reason
or security." [5] And later, "Lewis is weak at the point
of redemption precisely because his understanding of
evil and of man is lacking in dynamism and complexity. He fails to see that *redemption can never be
the same thing as unfallen innocence.*" [6] They find
Lewis's evil characters in *Strength* unconvincing.

---

[3] Ibid., p. 62.
[4] Fyodor Dostoyevsky, "Notes from Underground," in *The
Short Novels of Dostoyevsky* (New York: The Dial Press,
1945), p. 149.
[5] Rose and Rose, *The Shattered Ring,* p. 66.
[6] Ibid., p. 67.

75

It is difficult to take the evil they represent very seriously. They all seem to verge on utter madness and their intellectual circumlocutions tend to amount to rank stupidity. . . . [they] are just plain nasty — the kind of people children are warned against in the vague hints of grownups. [7]

Thus the Roses' reaction to Lewis — which I think is sufficiently typical of one sort of modern reaction to be worth careful analysis — may be summed up as follows: "Lewis's good characters are "passive," "docile," "static," do not have the essential "dynamism" the Roses admire and demand. Lewis's "good races" are not "fiercely life affirming," they "drift in . . . conflictless bliss . . . nestled against the benevolent bosom of nature." They are characterized by "instinctive docility." The evil characters are mere caricatures, bogeymen to frighten children.

By following up these three accusations we gain, I hope, a valuable insight into Lewis's real views and even some of the techniques he uses. Consider first the accusation of "passivity" and "docility." In one sense the accusation simply seems to be false. For example, Ransom's adventure in *Silent Planet* may be roughly summarized as follows:

Benighted on a walking tour, Ransom, because of a promise to a chance-met woman, forces his way into the villains' headquarters where he secures the release of the woman's half-witted son. Tricked and drugged by the villains, he almost manages to escape, but is recaptured and kidnaped to Mars by spaceship. On landing, he escapes at the first opportunity and manages to live off the land for several days. He meets and makes friends with a Martian and lives for some time in a Martian village, learning the language. With his Martian friends he goes on a hunt for a deadly water-

---

[7] Ibid., p. 64.

monster, which he assists in killing. When the villains catch up with him and kill one of his Martian friends, he voluntarily undertakes a dangerous journey to be judged for his part in the tragedy by the Martian "government," which he still fears and distrusts to some extent. After the "court of inquiry" — at which he uses his knowledge of the language to interpret for his kidnapers — Ransom is given the choice of staying on Mars or making a desperate dash for Earth with his former captors. He survives the dangerous journey and arrives safely home.

Such an outline gives no real idea of the excellences of *Silent Planet*, but it is plain that purely on the level of events Ransom is as "active" a hero as most. He is not a "superhero," but a believable character whose successes are well within the realm of possibility. Similar defenses could be made of some of the good characters in *Strength*. So if the Roses' accusations of "docility," "lack of dynamism," etc., have any truth, it must be on a somewhat different level.

To see what is really bothering the Roses, let us turn to their similar accusations against the unfallen Malacandrans and the Perelandrans whose fall is averted. Lewis's actual scheme here is rather complex. Let me summarize it briefly:

The Old Worlds (Mars and by implication perhaps other such worlds) contain races which are good and happy, but not entirely independent. They are in the care of powerful spirits — angels in fact — who direct and guide them. In certain cases these beings directly interfere to help or punish. Thus it is true in a way that the Martians are like children under guardianship.

Earth is the turning point, the first world where the "experiment" of complete independence was tried. Far from helping or guiding or directing humanity to good, the angels "assigned" to Earth are in rebellion

77

against God. This is one factor in a situation in which man in the person of his representatives is given a choice of following God's laws freely without guardianship or of rejecting God and making himself his god. Man has failed this test (the Fall), but God, by the Incarnation and Redemption, has turned this apparent defeat into a new sort of victory. One of the consequences of this is that God now acts *through* men who are members of his "mystical body," the Christian church. Ransom thus bears an awesome responsibility; if he fails, as man's first parents and representatives failed, God may again have to intervene in some unforeseeable way. The "bent" (evil) chief angel of our world (Satan) must also act through a representative; but whereas Ransom is left on his own (even having to partly figure out the problem and its solution for himself), Satan's representative, formerly the scientist Weston, is now a mere puppet manipulated by Satan, his own personality superseded and almost destroyed.

Perelandra is the first of the New Worlds. By successfully passing the test that Adam and Eve failed on our world, the Green Lady and the King enter into a new relation with the angels and with nature. Far from being under the guardianship of angels, they are to give orders to them; far from "nestling on the bosom of nature," they are to take complete charge of even the natural processes of growth, change of seasons, etc. The descendants of the King and the Green Lady are eventually to take some part in the "liberation" of our world at the Second Coming of Christ, which will not be — as we tend to think of it — "the end," but the *real* beginning for man.

Lewis has used basic elements of the Christian religion (the Fall, the Redemption, the Second Coming) which he fully believes, together with mythical elements (such as the Neoplatonic idea that the planets are moved and directed by angels) which are merely the "machinery" of the story. He is not recommending a return to the condition of the Old Worlds which are "under guardianship"; to this extent he agrees with the Roses that it is false that "never to have fallen is equivalent to redemption." But there are two ways of being "unfallen." The Malacandrans show one way: not fallen because protected from falling. But the Perelandrans show another way of being unfallen: they have faced temptation and overcome it. This is not to be sheltered or docile; as Lewis says, the evil live sheltered lives by giving in to temptation. They haven't the least idea of the difficulty of resisting a temptation for hours or days or weeks.

But we cannot go forward to the state of "successfully unfallen" Perelandra any more than we can go back to the guardianship under which Malacandra is ruled. Our state is that of fallen but redeemed man, with the consequence that if God's work is to be done at all, it must be done by us; not by angels, not by miraculous intervention, but by our own stumbling and flawed efforts. This is far from a call to "passivity."

One thing we must not do is use the tools of our opponents in trying to do God's work (as Christians, tragically, have so often done). As Ransom says in *Strength*:

> I am not allowed to be *too* prudent. I am not allowed to use desperate remedies until desperate diseases are really apparent. Otherwise we become just like our enemies — breaking all the rules whenever we imagine that it might possibly do some vague good to humanity in the far future. [8]

In one of the subtler passages in *Strength*, Lewis shows how the villains expect their opponents to try to succeed by the same means — political power, in-

_____
[8] Lewis, *That Hideous Strength* (New York: The Macmillan Co., 1965), p. 145.

fluence, money — that they themselves use. Mark Studdock, in a sense the "hero" of *Strength*, is suspected by the villains' organization, the N.I.C.E., of being in contact with "the enemy." An officer of N.I.C.E. "institutional police" explains why he had certain possible "contacts" followed, but not Dimble, the actual representative of Ransom's organization at St. Anne's.

He was shadowed into Northumberland. Only three possible people left the College after him — Lancaster, Lyly, and Dimble. I put them in that order of probability. Lancaster is a Christian, and a very influential man. He's in the Lower House of Convocation. He had a lot to do with the Repton Conference. He's mixed up with several big clerical families. And he's written a lot of books. He has a real stake in their side. Lyly is rather the same type, but less of an organizer. As you will remember, he did a great deal of harm on that reactionary commission about Education last year. Both these are dangerous men. They are the sort of people who get things done — natural leaders of the other party. Dimble is quite a different type. Except that he's a Christian, there isn't really much against him. He's purely academic. I shouldn't think his name is much known, except to other scholars in his own subject. Not the kind that would make a public man. Impractical . . . he'd be too full of scruples to be much use to them. The others know a thing or two, Lancaster particularly. In fact, he's a man we could find room for on our own side if he held the right views. [9]

Notice that the evil characters essentially expect their opponents to be like themselves, for example, to be unable to use Dimble because of his "scruples." The N.I.C.E. crew apparently see their opponents simply as another power-hungry group, with different

[9] Ibid., p. 237.

vested interests, competing for power and influence. As we shall see, Tolkien also makes use of this inability of the evil forces to really understand the nature of their opponents as an important plot element in the *Ring* trilogy.

However, I think the Roses' uneasiness does have an explanation. When they say that in Lewis's view "a perfect world is based on hierarchical principles," they may mean any of several things. If they mean that Lewis's view is that man ought to be subordinated to superior angelic beings, as the Malacandrans are, they are simply mistaken, as we have seen. If they mean that Lewis is not in one sense a strict egalitarian, this is true enough, but a side issue. As *Strength* makes clear, Lewis's view is that "we must all be guarded by equal rights from one another's greed, because we are fallen . . . [but] equality is not the deepest thing" (p. 148). Jane Studdock is offended because Ivy Maggs, her former cleaning woman, is accepted as an equal member of the company at St. Anne's. But this democracy goes with a recognition that certain persons are spiritually superior to others and a recognition that certain kinds of authority derive ultimately from God. Ransom is "Director" at St. Anne's, both because the others recognize his spiritual superiority and because the eldils have given him a certain task — a task which is "God's work" — in a very literal sense.

Subordination to angels is not Lewis's ideal, then, and subordination to better men than ourselves is something voluntary and exceptional. But if the Roses mean by a "hierarchical" view that man ought to be subordinate to God, then, of course, this is Lewis's view and the view, one would suppose, of any Christian theist. For surely there are only three possibilities: (1) God does not exist, and thus no question of obeying Him arises; (2) God exists and is to be obeyed;

(3) God exists, but is not to be obeyed. The first of these alternatives is a typical modern view, the second is the traditional Christian view. But what is to be made of the third? If Christianity is true, then God is perfectly wise and perfectly loving. To choose His will is to choose joy for ourselves and for others; to reject His will is to reject this joy. It is certainly possible to choose something other than the will of God, but this choice, on the Christian view, is precisely what sin consists of. To admit the Christian idea of God and reject the idea of obedience to Him, is, in effect, to be a Satanist. Thus it would seem that the Roses' rejection of the "hierarchical principle" is either a rejection of Christianity or is based on one of the misunderstandings which we have discussed.

But, one might ask, is it not possible to reject the will of God and still be in many ways good or admirable? The Christian answer is "in the long run, no," and this is the clue that enables us to understand Lewis's treatment of his villains. The traditional Christian view, forcefully expressed by Lewis, is that whatever excellences a creature may have are gifts from God; by cutting oneself off from God one ultimately loses *everything* good. The evil characters in *Strength* represent the end result of this process. They have lost, almost, their basic humanity; they are caricatures, but as in all successful caricatures, the elements which are exaggerated are essential elements. Lewis's attitude towards them is that very few human beings ever actually reach such an extreme stage of separation from goodness, but it is possible for them to do so. Lewis says in his paper "The Weight of Glory,"

> It is a serious thing to live in a society of possible gods and goddesses, to remember that the dullest and most uninteresting person you talk to may one day be a creature which, if you saw it now, you would

82

be strongly tempted to worship, or else a horror and a corruption such as you now meet, if at all, only in a nightmare. [10]

In a way, *Strength* is such a nightmare. The purpose of Wither, Frost, and Hardcastle is like that of a *memento mori*, without the inevitability; you or I may come to this, but need not.

There is some evidence that the Roses disagree with this whole point of view. "Such a conception of man," they say, speaking of Lewis's view,

is a bit arbitrary; it ignores the possibility that man is an indivisible unity, not to mention the insight of psychoanalysis that man's strengths and weaknesses may be one and the same, that the strongest positive characteristics carry with them the strongest negative possibilities. [11]

Like so much the Roses say, this is open to two quite different interpretations. Lewis would readily admit that "the strongest positive characteristics carry with them the strongest negative possibilities." As Lewis has George MacDonald say in *The Great Divorce:*

There's something in natural affection which will lead it on to eternal love more easily than natural appetite could be led on. But there's also something in it which makes it easier to stop at the natural level and mistake it for the heavenly. Brass is mistaken for gold more easily than clay is. And if it finally refuses conversion its corruption will be worse than the corruption of what ye call the lower passions. It's a stronger angel and therefore, when it falls, a fiercer devil. [12]

---

[10] "The Weight of Glory" in *The Weight of Glory and Other Addresses* (Grand Rapids: Wm. B. Eerdmans Publishing Co., 1949), p. 15.

[11] Rose and Rose, *The Shattered Ring,* p. 63.

[12] *The Great Divorce* (New York: The Macmillan Co., 1946), p. 97.

However, in another sense, what the Roses mean may be diametrically opposed to what Lewis means. If they are suggesting that flaws or faults in our nature may be the source of strengths or excellences, or might be inseparable from them, Lewis would reject this view entirely. Evil, according to Lewis, is essentially uncreative. He has Screwtape say in *The Screwtape Letters,*

> To be greatly and effectively wicked a man needs some virtue. What would Attilla have been without his courage, or Shylock without self-denial as regards the flesh? But as we [i.e., Hell] cannot supply these qualities ourselves we can only use them as supplied by the Enemy [i.e., God] — and this means leaving Him a kind of foothold in those men whom, otherwise we have made most securely our own. [13]

And as Lewis has MacDonald say toward the end of *Divorce:* "Nothing, not even the best and noblest can go on as it is now. Nothing, not even what is lowest and most bestial, will not be raised again if it submits to death." [14] Thus the view that evil can be a source of any strength or excellence, or an irremovable part of any, would be totally rejected by Lewis.

The Roses cite the evidence of psychoanalysis, but all that any empirical study can show us is that good and evil are in fact mixed in man as he now exists. Man's ultimate destiny and the role of his virtues and vices in this destiny are matters for philosophy and religion.

Besides showing personal character at the extreme stage of separation from goodness, Lewis also shows a society as it becomes at such an extreme. In *Screwtape* Lewis discusses the problems of depicting the relations of devils to each other.

---

[13] *The Screwtape Letters* (New York: The Macmillan Co.), pp. 135-36.
[14] *The Great Divorce*, p. 104.

Milton has told us that "devil with devil damned, Firm concord holds." But how? Certainly not by friendship. A being which can still love is not yet a devil. Here again my symbol [Hell as "something like the bureaucracy of a police state or the offices of a thoroughly nasty business concern"] seemed to me useful. It enabled me, by earthly parallels to picture an official society held together entirely by fear and greed. . . . "Dog eat dog" is the principle of the whole organization. Everyone wishes everyone else's discrediting, demotion and ruin; everyone is an expert in the confidential report, the pretended alliance, the stab in the back.[15]

Lewis was even more successful in the depiction of such a society in *Strength* than he was in *Screwtape*. The way in which Mark Studdock is bamboozled by Wither, betrayed by Feverstone, snubbed by Steele, used by Cosser, bullied and blackmailed by Hardcastle, and "trained" by Frost gives a vivid picture of the way in which such a society would appear to a neophyte. The devious atmosphere of lies and double-cross is illustrated by many fine touches. For example, at a time when Studdock is locked in a cell, still being terrified and threatened by Frost and Wither, his name is being used to terrify others. The speech in which this occurs is a beautiful illustration of Wither's methods of terrorizing his subordinates.

Well, Mr. Stone, I am, on the whole, and with certain inevitable reservations, moderately satisfied with your conduct of this affair. I believe that I may be able to present it in a favorable light to those of my colleagues whose good will you have, unfortunately, been able to retain. If you could bring it to a successful conclusion, you would very much strengthen your position. If not . . . it is inexpressibly painful to me that there should be these tensions and mutual recriminations among us. But you quite understand

15 *The Screwtape Letters*, pp. x, xi.

me, my dear boy. If only I could persuade — say Miss Hardcastle and Mr. Studdock — to share my appreciation of your very real qualities, you would need to have no apprehensions about your career or — ah — your security. [16]

In contrast, the society at St. Anne's, the headquarters of Ransom and his companions, is one based on mutual respect and affection, which extends even to the bear, Bultitude. Things as minor as household chores are shared.

"What is 'women's day' in the kitchen?" asked Jane of Mother Dimble.

"There are no servants here," said Mother Dimble, "and we do all the work. The women do it one day and the men the next. What? No it's a very sensible arrangement. The Director's idea is that men and women can't do housework together without quarreling. There's something in it. Of course it doesn't do to look at the cups too closely on the men's day, but on the whole we get along pretty well." [17]

Dangers, too, are shared, as on the night of the hunt for Merlin. Only MacPhee is denied a share because his lack of Christian faith leaves him too exposed to the forces of evil. MacPhee, incidentally, is an interesting part of the company at St. Anne's. A nonbeliever, he is the "official sceptic" of the establishment. His allegiance to the company is based partly on affection for Ransom, partly on detestation for the evil at Belbury. MacPhee is partly an affectionate caricature of Lewis's old tutor, partly a personification of nineteenth century rationalism, which tried to reject religion while retaining morality. But like other great Lewis characters (Reepicheep the mouse, for

---

16 Lewis, *That Hideous Strength*, pp. 252-53.
17 Ibid., p. 167.

example, or Puddleglum the Marsh-wiggle, or Augray the sorn) he is, whatever his origin, a successful result of artistic creation.

Indeed, I suspect that part of the indignation some moderns feel about Lewis — their accusations that he writes "propaganda" or, absurdly, "a formal apology for Christianity" — is that he applies one of their own techniques in reverse. The modern temper has been fed to some extent on works in which the pleasant characters represent science, progress, political leftism, and so on, and the unpleasant characters represent religion, absolute ethical values, tradition, and so on. H. G. Wells is a vintage source of this kind of technique. But in Lewis the allocations of virtue and vice are reversed. No one in his right mind would want to be part of the "society" at Belbury, and it requires very strong prejudices indeed not to be attracted by the company at St. Anne's.

But whereas people like Wells did almost seem to be saying that "progressives" are Nice People and "reactionaries" are Nasty People, Lewis is not saying that Christians are Nice People and scientists are Nasty People. He is saying that morally good people, people who *act* on the Christian principles of love and justice — even if, like MacPhee, they are honest unbelievers — are people it is good to be among; and morally evil people, whose lives are based on self-love and hatred of others — even if, like Straik, they use the language of religion — are people it is bad to be among. And this is true as a matter of experience, even if it were not almost true by definition.

Why, then, does anyone adhere to Belbury rather than St. Anne's? Because he thinks he can use Belbury to secure some aim of his own. Consider some sample motives from the Belbury crew:

Feverstone: "He knew that the Belbury scheme might not work, but he knew that if it didn't he would get out in time. He had a dozen lines of retreat kept open. He also had a perfectly clear conscience and had played no tricks with his mind. He had never slandered another man except to get his job, never cheated except because he wanted money, never really disliked people unless they bored him." [18]

Wither: "He had long since ceased to believe in knowledge itself. What had been in his far-off youth a merely aesthetic repugnance to realities that were crude or vulgar had deepened and darkened, year after year, into a fixed refusal of anything that was in any degree other than himself. [19]

Mark Studdock is nearly drawn into the orbit of Belbury by the craving which Lewis has analyzed in "The Inner Ring" (collected in *The Weight of Glory*). Studdock has always longed to be an "insider," in the "inner ring" of the knowledgeable powerful who "really run things," "really know what's going on." This craving leads him from the "Progressive Element" at Bracton to the N.I.C.E. and even exerts a pull on him after his "conversion," when Frost tempts him with the vision of the ultimate "inner ring." The Satanist initiates, "For here, surely here at last . . . was the true inner circle of all, the circle whose centre was outside the human race — the ultimate secret, the supreme power, the last initiation." [20] But as an illustration of what Lewis has MacDonald say in *Divorce*, Mark's association with the old tramp he is set to guard contains in a way a satisfaction of what was legitimate in Mark's desire.

Mark never noticed until years later that here, where there was no room for vanity and no more security than "children playing in a giant's kitchen," he had

[18] Ibid., p. 356.
[19] Ibid., p. 353.
[20] Ibid., p. 259.

unawares become a member of a "circle" as secret and as strongly fenced from outsiders as any that he had dreamed of. [21]

By the end of the book, Mark Studdock has undergone a fundamental change in his attitude, but he is still taking only the first faltering steps back to full humanity. Lewis's fully developed good characters offer a more instructive contrast to the Belbury crew.

Ransom himself is hard to come to grips with, since for much of *Silent Planet* and *Perelandra* he is simply Everyman. We see the action through his eyes, know his innermost fears and weaknesses, and find ourselves identifying with him so strongly that it is hard to give an objective estimate of him. Perhaps the outstanding impression we carry away is that Ransom is "open" — able to appreciate and love. He delights in the beauty of Mars, grows to love the *hross* and especially Hyoi, his first friend among them. After overcoming his initial fear of the sorns he begins to appreciate their wisdom, their humor, even their physical beauty. On Perelandra his struggles, temptations, and victories are such as we can make our own: we hope that we would do as well as Ransom in his place, fear that we would do worse. Humility, charity, and courage are not easy characteristics to convey — we find them all in Ransom.

There are two pictures of Ransom from the "outside" in Perelandra, both by "Lewis," who appears as a minor character in the story. Before Ransom's trip to Perelandra, his humanity and decency are emphasized. After his return Ransom seems "larger than life." He is "almost a new Ransom, glowing with health and rounded with muscle and seemingly ten years younger. In the old days he had been beginning to show a few grey hairs; but now the beard which

---

21 Ibid., p. 313.

swept his chest was pure gold." [22] To Ransom, returned from Perelandra, ordinary earthpeople appear pale and sick, which indirectly emphasizes his own vigor and energy.

Thus transfigured Ransom prepares us for the Ransom of *Strength*. Although a somewhat remote figure, as we have noted, he shows humor, wisdom, and sympathy in his interview with Jane Studdock. At her first sight of him he "appeared to be a boy, twenty years old." But he soon realized that

> of course he was not a boy — how could she have thought so? The fresh skin on his forehead and cheeks and, above all, on his hands, had suggested the idea. But no boy could have so full a beard. And no boy could be so strong. She had expected to see an invalid. Now it was manifest that the grip of those hands would be inescapable, and imagination suggested that those arms and shoulders could support the whole house. Miss Ironwood at her side struck her as a little old woman, shrivelled and pale — a thing you could have blown away. [23]

Again, the contrast between Ransom and other "normal" persons gives us an impression of Ransom's power. Ransom's face, young but wise, with its golden beard, arouses images in Jane's mind, "the imagined Arthur of her childhood — and the imagined Solomon, too. Solomon — for the first time in many years the bright solar blend of king and lover and magician which hangs about that name stole back upon her mind. For the first time in all those years she tasted the word *King* itself with all linked associations of battle, marriage, priesthood, mercy, and power." [24]

---

[22] Lewis, *Perelandra* (New York: The Macmillan Co., n.d.), p. 128.

[23] Lewis, *That Hideous Strength*, p. 142.

[24] Lewis, *That Hideous Strength*, pp. 142-43.

But the effect of this meeting on Jane is moral, not merely physical. Her talk with him begins to make her more like Ransom. Before the meeting she travels on a small train.

Passengers got in and out of her carriage at every stop; apple-faced men, and women with elastic-side boots and imitation fruit on their hats, and school-boys. Jane hardly noticed them; for though she was theoretically an extreme democrat, no social class save her own had yet become a reality to her in any place except the printed page. [25]

After the interview, returning on the same train,

She saw from the windows of the train the outlined beams of sunlight pouring over stubble or burnished woods and felt that they were like the notes of a trumpet. Her eyes rested on the rabbits and cows as they flitted by and she embraced them in heart with merry, holiday love. She delighted in the oc-casional speech of the one wizened old man who shared her compartment and saw, as never before, the beauty of his shrewd and sunny old mind, sweet as a nut and English as a chalk down. She reflected with surprise how long it was since music had any part in her life, and resolved to listen to many chorales by Bach on the gramophone that evening. Or else — perhaps — she would read a great many Shakespeare sonnets. She rejoiced also in her hunger and thirst and decided that she would make herself buttered toast for tea — a great deal of buttered toast. [26]

For Lewis, this is no parable or symbol, but the plain truth: as we come closer to God, either in Him-self or through His servants, we will grow in love and delight, in appreciation of all good things.

---

[25] Ibid., p. 50.
[26] Ibid., p. 152.

Perhaps the second most important of Lewis's "good" characters is Lucy, heroine of several of the Narnia books. Lucy's character grows in the three books in which she appears, as she herself grows in loving and serving Aslan, the Christ-figure of the Narnia stories. Lucy is the first of the children to discover Narnia and has to suffer a sort of martyrdom when she is not at first believed. Her immediate friendliness to Tumnus the faun, her grave courtesy to all the Narnian creatures, reminds us of Alice. Even though she has suffered from Edmund's cruelty, she is the first to plead with Aslan to help him. She knows that Edmund should know the sacrifice that Aslan has made for him, when Susan thinks "it would be too awful for him" to know. She is not, of course, perfect. For example, she snaps at Aslan when worried about Edmund's wounds. But she is growing.

Her reward is to be asked to do more. In *Prince Caspian*, at a crucial turn in the story only she can see Aslan and must persuade the others to follow him on her word alone. In *The Voyage of the Dawn Treader* she sacrifices her water ration to the unpleasant Eustace and undertakes to break the spell on the Dufflepuds. And she is growing in knowledge and love of Aslan. When she meets him in *Prince Caspian*:

"Aslan," said Lucy, "you're bigger."

"That is because you are older, little one," answered he.

"Not because you are?"

"I am not. But every year you grow, you will find me bigger." [27]

In *Dawn Treader* Lucy is dismayed to find that she cannot return to Narnia.

[27] Lewis, *Prince Caspian* (New York: The Macmillan Co., 1951), p. 124.

"It isn't Narnia you know" sobbed Lucy, "It's you. We shan't meet you there. And how can we live, never meeting you?"

"But you shall meet me, dear one," said Aslan.

"Are — are you there too, Sir?" said Edmund.

"I am" said Aslan. "But there I have another name. You must learn to know me by that name. This was the very reason why you were brought to Narnia, that by knowing me here for a little, you may know me better there." [28]

Even more true to life in some ways than Ransom and Lucy are the characters who change from evil to good. We have already mentioned Mark Studdock. Eustace in *Dawn Treader* is reformed by the rather drastic expedient of turning him temporarily into a dragon. The objectification of his inner repulsiveness, as well as the kindness of those whom he had thought his persecutors, accomplishes a change in his character. But he has relapses in *The Silver Chair*, and even in Paradise, at the end of *The Last Battle*, some of his old bumptiousness is left.

All in all, the characters whom Lewis intends us to admire are an attractive crew. Some of their characteristics, like Ransom's health and vigor after his return from Perelandra, are merely symbolic. Health, which is a physical good, is used as a symbol for moral goodness. But the traits which make these characters basically attractive are just those which attract us to people in real life — concern, respect, and affection for others, humility, courage, openness to experience, and appreciation of all good things. And for Lewis, the connection between these characteristics is clear. God's goodness is the source of all good things, leaving no room for conceit on our part. Each good gift should

[28] Lewis, *The Voyage of the Dawn Treader* (New York: The Macmillan Co., 1952), p. 207.

remind us of the Giver and motivate us to imitate God's goodness by doing good to others. On the other hand, the pride, selfishness, and cruelty illustrated in Lewis's evil characters all arise from the fatal choice of self instead of God — the impossible attempt to be sufficient unto ourselves and to dominate others with our ideas and wishes. Lewis gives a modern version of Augustine's "two cities" — the Manor at St. Anne's, founded on love of God, and Belbury, founded on love of self.

chapter 5

Good and Evil
in Tolkien

Both Lewis and Tolkien, as we said in the last chapter, are Christians, and their morality is essentially Christian morality. This is so clear in Lewis that we have found critics accusing him of propaganda. It is much less clear in Tolkien, and this has tempted some critics to say that Tolkien's view of the world is "really" the modern view and not the traditional Christian view. This is so major a misunderstanding of Tolkien that the Roses' misunderstanding of Lewis pales into insignificance by comparison. The motives of this misunderstanding are revealing enough of a certain modern tendency to make them worth examining carefully.

One major critic of Tolkien who has made this mistake is Roger Sale.[1] According to Sale, Tolkien may wish it differently, but

---

[1] Sale's thesis is set forth in a study called "England's Parnassus," first published in the *Hudson Review* and later expanded and revised for a book of Tolkien criticism, *Tolkien and the Critics,* ed. Neil D. Isaacs and Rose A. Zimbardo (Notre Dame, Ind.: University of Notre Dame Press, 1968).

willy nilly he belongs to our time, and the more he attempts to ignore or escape this fact the worse he becomes as a writer. . . . He is a Christian, not a sceptic, and he believes that the taproot to the past is not yet dried or withered. It would be difficult, therefore, to expect that Tolkien would warm to the idea that his imagination is vastly superior to his theology and that his imagination is of his own time. . . . the heroism he writes of best is very modern. [2]

What does Sale mean by "modern heroism"? It "accepts the facts of modern life . . . and simply refuses to knuckle under" (p. 284). Again:

We see without in the least needing to make the seeing into a formulation, what the heroism of our time is and can be: lonely, lost, scared, loving, willing, and compassionate — to bind oneself to the otherness of others by recognizing our common livingness. History may create the condition of chaos, but man's nature is to reply to history as well as to acknowledge it. [3]

Now certainly Tolkien describes such a view, but it is not *his* view, it is the view of Northern mythology. Tolkien writes in "Beowulf: the Monsters and the Critics" and in "The Homecoming of Beorhtnoth, Beorhthelm's Son" about this view. [4] It is a view which Tolkien respects and in a way admires. But to confuse it with Tolkien's own view or with that expressed in the *Ring* trilogy is a major error.

The corrective, in fact, is in the very sources where Tolkien discusses the view. In "Monsters" Tolkien says,

---

[2] Isaacs and Zimbardo, eds., *Tolkien and the Critics,* p. 248.
[3] Ibid., p. 288.
[4] "Beowulf: the Monsters and the Critics" in *An Anthology of Beowulf Criticism,* ed. Lewis E. Nicholson (Notre Dame, Ind.: University of Notre Dame Press, 1963); "The Homecoming of Beorhtnoth, Beorhthelm's Son" in *The Tolkien Reader* (New York: Ballantine Books, 1966).

Now the heroic figures, the men of old . . . remained and still fought on until defeat. For the monsters do not depart, whether the gods go or come. A Christian was (and is) still like his forefathers, a mortal hemmed in a hostile world. The monsters remained the enemies of mankind, the infantry of the old war, and become inevitably the enemies of the one God . . . the eternal Captain of the new. Even so the vision of the war changes. For it begins to dissolve, even as the contest on the fields of Time thus takes on its largest aspect. The tragedy of the great temporal defeat remains for a while poignant, but ceases to be finally important. It is no defeat, for the end of the world is part of the design of Metod, the Arbiter who is above the mortal world. Beyond there appears a possibility of eternal victory (or eternal defeat) and the real battle is between the soul and its adversaries. So the old monsters become images of the evil spirit or spirits. [5]

Tolkien is here describing the situation of the Beowulf poet who, as modern scholarship has established, was a Christian writing at the time of Bede (ca. A.D. 675) but deliberately excluding explicitly Christian elements from a tale which is supposed to take place at a time before Christ. The situation of the Beowulf poet is a very close parallel to Tolkien's own situation, as we will see, and he has partly learned from the Beowulf poet how to handle it.

Sale has an answer to this answer: Sale knows better than Tolkien what Tolkien "really" means. Sale knows this, he claims, because Tolkien's "imagination" is modern; he sees heroism in essentially modern terms. It may be worth spelling out why this is precisely false. The ideal which Sale has in mind is roughly existentialist stoicism as we find it in Sartre and Camus. The world is chaotic and absurd, we must refuse all

---

[5] "Beowulf: the Monsters and the Critics," loc. cit., pp. 72-73.

easy ways out — suicide, religion, other forms of self-delusion — and impose our own meaning on life, with undeviating determination. This is an ideal by no means devoid of a certain "wintry grandeur" (as Lewis said of Sartre), but it is a million miles from Tolkien's vision. What Lewis said of Spenser is equally true of Tolkien.

> The Existentialist feels Angst because he thinks that man's nature (and therefore his relation to all things) has to be created or invented, without guidance, at each moment of decision. Spenser thought that man's nature was given, discoverable, and discovered; he did not feel Angst. He was often sad: but not, at bottom, worried.[6]

Frodo in The Lord of the Rings is facing not chaos, but a definite evil, which is evil by absolute standards. "Good and ill have not changed . . . nor are they one thing among Elves and Dwarves and another among Men."[7] He is not imposing his own will or his own vision, but defending a law and a vision common to elves, men, and dwarves. Bilbo's finding of the Ring and his bearing of it are not chance events, but part of a great plan, prophesied in part and known to the Wise. It would be hard in some ways to find a hero more unlike the existentialist hero.

Obviously Frodo is "lonely, lost, scared"; that is the sort of hero he is: not a Beowulf or even a Gawain, but a Jack the Giant Killer, the "youngest son," "the simple one" never expected to succeed but succeeding at last with the aid of courage, resourcefulness, luck, and powerful helpers. Not that Tolkien despises the other sort of hero; Gandalf, Aragon, Legolas, and

---

[6] Lewis, English Literature in the Sixteenth Century Excluding Drama (New York: Oxford University Press, 1954), p. 392.

[7] Tolkien, The Two Towers, rev. ed. (New York: Ballantine Books, 1969), pp. 40-41.

Gimli are all variations of that traditional type. But Tolkien's real love, and ours, is for Bilbo and Frodo, Sam, Pippin, and Merry.

Another critic who makes a mistake about Tolkien similar to Sale's is Charles Moorman. His essay, "'Now Entertain Conjecture of a Time' — The Fictive Worlds of C. S. Lewis and J. R. R. Tolkien," is to be found in another excellent collection of papers, *Shadows of Imagination*, edited by Mark R. Hillegas. Moorman also wants to say that Tolkien's vision is not Christian, but whereas Sale calls it "modern," Moorman's word is "pagan." He says that

> in spite of Tolkien's own implication in "On Fairy-Stories" that *The Lord of the Rings*, ending as it does in a "sudden joyous turn," . . . possesses eucatas-trophe and is hence by extension optimistic and Christian, I would maintain that it reflects the at-titudes and interests of Tolkien the student of Beo-wulf rather than those of Tolkien the Christian. The chronicles . . . are filled with accounts of never-ceas-ing wars against evil waged by elves, hobbits and men, and the reappearance in every age of the forces of darkness. . . . Though the forces of good triumph in each age their leaders pay a high cost for victory . . . the scars cannot be erased. . . . The views of nature and civilization like those of history and the individual life advanced in *The Lord of the Rings* seem to be pagan rather than Christian in essence. [8]

This view of Moorman's seems to rest on a double misunderstanding of Christianity and of Tolkien. The "sudden joyous turn," the "eucatastrophe" of the Chris-tian Story that Tolkien cites in "On Fairy-Stories," is the Resurrection, not the end of the world. And Christ's victory does not mean that suffering and the battle with evil are over; it means that we must each take up our cross and follow in the footsteps of Christ.

---

[8] Carbondale, Ill.: Southern Illinois University Press, pp. 64-65.

The world has been saved, but we must work out that salvation, sometimes in fear and trembling.

Moorman cites the contrasting atmosphere of Lewis's Narnia stories, where the heroes and heroines seem to emerge relatively unscathed and the victory of good seems more complete. But of course, Lewis's stories were written for children and cannot contain the full weight of sorrow and sin that a story for older readers can. Furthermore, the machinery of the stories requires that, at the end of each book except the last, the children who are the heroes and heroines must return to being children in our world. And though the victory in each book seems more complete, each new adventure into Narnia is a fresh battle against evil. The victory of evil in the last book seems complete, until the "sudden joyous turn," which is the end of Narnia and the good news that the children are really dead in our world and can live forever with Aslan.

Furthermore, Moorman does not seem to have fully grasped Tolkien's view. He cites the fact that Frodo, wounded and sorrowful, must pass from Middle-earth. But he goes to the land of the High Elves, there to to be cured of all wounds and sorrows. Similarly, Ransom, at the end of The Hideous Strength, leaves Earth to return to Perelandra, for only there can his wound be healed.

In fact, Tolkien and Lewis both have a profoundedly Christian view: this world is the vale of sorrow and struggle, and we must look for real consolation only after death or after the world ends. G. K. Chesterton expresses this view in verse.

> Here we have battle and blazing eyes
> And chance and honor and high surprise
> But our homes are under impossible skies
> Where the yule tale was begun. [9]

[9] "The House of Christmas" in Collected Poems (London: Methuen, 1935).

Both Sale and Moorman genuinely admire Tolkien, and their attempt to restate his vision in their own terms arises from that admiration. But Tolkien's vision is profoundly his own and deeply Christian, and if we misunderstand this we seriously misunderstand him.

Let me now briefly describe Tolkien's world, as many hints, indirect references, and direct statements give it to us. Just as in Lewis's space trilogy the state of Earth is supposed to be the state it is in, and Lewis's secondary world "starts," so to speak, at the orbit of the moon, so for Tolkien recorded history is supposed to be much as it actually is, and Tolkien's secondary world "starts" before history begins. In both cases there is some "interpenetration." In *Strength* the Arthurian legend becomes history, and in Tolkien it is suggested that elves, hobbits, and other creatures linger on into recorded history. But before recorded history there are certain events which Tolkien, as a Christian, holds to have actually occurred — for instance, the fall of man. Thus, since there are men in Tolkien's story, they must be fallen men; the Fall is in the *past* of Tolkien's world. And, of course, the men in the story of the Ring are obviously fallen men.

What about the other races? Not being "sons of Adam," they are not necessarily fallen; they may be like Lewis's Malacandrans or Perelandrans. And, in fact, there are some analogies between Lewis's "races" and Tolkien's. Let me first give a table of my proposed correspondences, and then defend it.

Tolkien's	correspond to	Lewis's
Elves (wizards)	″	Good eldils (Oyarses)
Dwarves (ents?)	″	Malacandrans
Orcs, trolls (Sauron)	″	"Bent" eldils (The "Bent One")

Elves and orcs are unlike eldils in that eldils are purely spiritual beings. (But the function of elves in Tolkien's story is like that of eldils in Lewis's trilogy as, for example, Tom Bombadil's function is rather like Merlin's in *Strength*.) Elves are like eldils in being confirmed in goodness or badness; there is no such thing as an evil elf of a good orc in Tolkien. Ents are evidently not confirmed in goodness like elves. Treebeard says of his people,

> "I do not understand all that goes on myself, so I cannot explain it to you. Some of us are still true Ents, and lively enough in our fashion, but many are growing sleepy, going treeish, as you might say. Most of the trees are just trees, of course; but many are half awake. Some are quite wide awake, and a few are, well, ah, well getting *Entish*. That is going on all the time.

> "When that happens to a tree, you find that some have *bad* hearts. Nothing to do with their wood: I do not mean that. Why, I knew some good old willows down the Entwash, gone long ago, alas! They were quite hollow, indeed they were falling all to pieces, but as quiet and sweet-spoken as a young leaf. And then there are some trees in the valleys under the mountains, sound as a bell, and bad right through. That sort of thing seems to spread. There used to be some very dangerous parts in this country. There are still some very black patches." [10]

However, the ents have an "anti-race," like the elves. Treebeard says, "Maybe you have heard of Trolls? They are mighty strong. But Trolls are only counterfeits, made by the Enemy in the Great Darkness in mockery of Ents, as Orcs were of Elves." [11] This may suggest that trolls and orcs are actually *created* by the Enemy, but elsewhere Gandalf denies that the Enemy can create; he can only spoil and corrupt. In fact, "Nothing is evil in the beginning. Even Sauron was

---

[10] Tolkien, *The Two Towers*, pp. 88-89.
[11] Ibid., p. 113.

102

not so," [12] which suggests that he is, like Satan, a fallen being of great power.

Dwarves, like the Malacandrans, seem to be basically good, but there seems to be a possibility of individual falls; an evil dwarf is not an impossibility. And Gimli the dwarf in some way rises above his dwarvish destiny, becoming a sort of adopted elf.

Hobbits pose a special problem, and here I indulge in a bit of speculation which might have been entirely rejected by Tolkien himself. All that he himself says is that

> it is plain indeed that Hobbits are relatives of ours: far nearer to us than Elves, or even than Dwarves. Of old they spoke the languages of Men, after their own fashion, and liked and disliked much the same things as Men did. But what exactly our relationship is can no longer be discovered. [13]

However, the hobbits are continually referred to as "halflings," a term Tolkien explains as "half the size of a grown man." Can there also be some suggestion here of half-breeds? Can the hobbits in fact be the offspring of an interbreeding of two other races? If so, which two? Not elves and men. The offspring of such unions appear in the story in the persons of Elrond and Aragon, and they are quite unlike hobbits. I once thought hobbits might be the offspring of an elf-dwarf cross and connected in some way with the "old quarrel" between elves and dwarves. Gimli falls in love with Galadriel (in a remote and chivalric way, it is true, yet she is a sort of elvish saint or superwoman and he is not correspondingly great). What if some dwarvish king or warrior had fallen in love with a more eccessible elf-maiden and carried her off?

[12] Tolkien, *The Fellowship of the Ring*, rev. ed. (New York: Ballantine Books, 1969), p. 351.
[13] Ibid., pp. 20-21.

Might this not have led to a spreading quarrel (Helen of Troy long before Troy), and might not the offspring of such a union, perhaps intermarrying with other dwarves, have founded a new race who found it best to vanish quietly into a remote corner of the world?

I still think this possible, from what Tolkien tells us of his world, but I am now inclined to think that a mixed dwarf-human ancestry is more plausible in view of the part hobbits play in the story. For, if hobbits are partly human, much is explained: the fact that they have no language of their own but speak that of men; their resemblances to both men and dwarves in certain respects; and, above all, the vital role they play in the process in which the Third Age — the age of many "speaking races" — comes to an end, and the Fourth Age — the age of man — begins.

Be this as it may, the real moral focus of Tolkien's story is on the two races, hobbits and men. They can sink to complete damnation, as the Ringwraiths have done, and as Bilbo or Frodo might have. But they can rise to something like sanctity, as Frodo does. We have detailed pictures of moral struggle in men (Boromir, Théoden, Denethor), in most of the hobbit characters (especially Frodo, Sam, and Bilbo, but also Merry and Pippin), and in the wizard Saruman who is at least ostensibly a man or elf-man.

The constant temptation of all the characters is to give in, give up the struggle and cooperate with the Dark Lord. Against this the virtues characteristic of the heroes of the story are courage, will and endurance, and loyalty and love. We see the first sketch of this in Bilbo, hero of *The Hobbit*. At the beginning of the story he is seemingly a fussy, self-important little man (not middle-aged; that is a mistake which arises from applying human time-scales to longer-lived creatures). Partly by clever pressure from Gandalf, partly from injured vanity, he commits himself to an adventure with Thorin and his dwarves. As the dangers start, he begins to find his courage, first trying to pick a troll's pocket (with disastrous results), then giving the alarm during the capture by the goblins. Lost in the flight from the goblins after Gandalf rescues the troop, Bilbo meets Gollum and outwits him in the dark, finds his magic ring and begins to use it. In the forest he saves the dwarves from the giant spiders, aided by a magic ring and an elvish blade, but showing a great deal of courage and resourcefulness. He rescues the dwarves from the Elven-king's dungeons, but the real test of his courage is when he twice faces Smaug, the great dragon, gaining the knowledge that enables Bard, the hero, to kill the villain.

At the end of the tale, however, Bilbo shows his real stature. Faced with the refusal of the dwarves to share their wealth with the townsfolk against whom they aroused the dragon, and whose captain slew the dragon, Bilbo determines to see justice done. He gives the Arkenstone to the Elf-king and Bard to bargain with, then goes back to face the wrath of the dwarves. Love of justice and love of peace here raise Bilbo to a height not far below Frodo, the Ring-bearer.

Frodo rises to greater heights because from the beginning he accepts the burden of the Ring purely for the sake of others. It is no mere adventure that sends Frodo riding out of the Shire, but a willingness to suffer so that others may be saved — a willingness which is tested to the last grim degree on the black plains of Mordor. Frodo is not Christ, the Ring is not the Cross, and the salvation his sacrifice wins is a purely secular salvation. But there are obviously echoes of these greater realities in the fictional "Passion" of Frodo. "Greater love has no man than this, that a man lay down his life for his friends," says Christ, and Frodo's journey is at least an illustration of this.

The growth of Frodo in courage and loyalty is clear enough as the story develops. At the first real test, in the den of the Barrow-wight, he is tempted to use the Ring to save himself.

A wild thought of escape came to him. He wondered if he put on the Ring whether the Barrow-wight would miss him, and he might find some way out. He thought of himself running free over the grass, grieving for Merry, Sam, and Pippin, but free and alive himself. [14]

He rejects the temptation and begins to grow toward his final stature. There are other crises, and the Ring itself betrays him several times. But he is able to resist the call of the Ringwraiths to surrender on Weathertop and at the Ford of Bruinen, and to make up his own mind when assailed by the Enemy on Amon Hen.

. . . suddenly he felt the Eye. There was an eye in the Dark Tower that did not sleep. He knew that it had become aware of his gaze. A fierce eager will was there. It leaped towards him; almost like a finger he felt it, searching for him. Very soon it would nail him down, know just exactly where he was. Amon Lhaw it touched. It glanced upon Tol Brandir — he threw himself from the seat, crouching, covering his head with his grey hood.

He heard himself crying out: Never, never! Or was it: Verily I come, I come to you? He could not tell. Then as a flash from some other point of power there came to his mind another thought: Take it off! Take it off! Fool, take it off! Take off the Ring!

The two powers strove in him. For a moment, perfectly balanced between their piercing points, he writhed, tormented. Suddenly he was aware of him-

[14] Ibid., p. 195.

self again. Frodo, neither the Voice nor the Eye: free to choose, and with one remaining instant in which to do so. He took the Ring off his finger. He was kneeling in clear sunlight before the high seat. A black shadow seemed to pass like an arm above him; it missed Amon Hen and groped out west, and faded. Then all the sky was clean and blue and birds sang in every tree. [15]

Frodo grows even greater as he journeys on with Sam and Gollum. His gentleness to Gollum almost conquers the creature's withered heart, and his steady endurance of his burden as it grows almost overwhelming contains a moving echo of the Way of the Cross. Indeed, his nightmare journey across the blasted plains of Mordor with Sam and Gollum tends sometimes to dominate our memory of the book, so that it is easy to forget how much laughter and enchantment and delight the story contains.

Sam Gamgee's outstanding characteristics are his loyalty to Frodo and his love of Frodo; but Sam has his own complexities. His love of elves and his delight in the wonders they meet along the way reveal a streak of imagination and even of poetry. His dogged endurance is hinted at even in the beginning.

I seem to see ahead, in a kind of way. I know we are going to take a very long road, into darkness; but I know I can't turn back: It isn't to see Elves now, nor dragons, nor mountains, that I want — I don't rightly know what I want: but I have something to do before the end, and it lies ahead, not in the Shire. I must see it through, sir, if you understand me. [16]

At the end, when he and Frodo have accomplished their task and seem about to die, Sam urges the exhausted Frodo to one last effort.

[15] Ibid., p. 519.
[16] Ibid., pp. 126-27.

"I am glad that you are here with me," said Frodo. "Here at the end of all things, Sam."

"Yes, I am with you, Master," said Sam, laying Frodo's wounded hand gently to his breast. "And you're with me. And the journey's finished. But after coming all that way I don't want to give up yet. It's not like me, somehow, if you understand."

"Maybe not, Sam," said Frodo; "but it's like things are in the world. Hopes fail. And end comes. We have only a little time to wait now. We are lost in ruin and downfall, and there is no escape."

"Well, Master, we could at least go further from this dangerous place here, from this Crack of Doom, if that's its name. Now couldn't we? Come, Mr. Frodo, let's go down the path at any rate!"

"Very well, Sam. If you wish to go, I'll come," said Frodo; and they rose and went slowly down the winding road." [17]

Merry and Pippin at first show mainly their loyalty to Frodo.

"It all depends on what you want," put in Merry. "You can trust us to stick to you through thick and thin — to the bitter end. And you can trust us to keep any secret of yours — closer than you can keep it yourself. But you cannot trust us to let you face trouble alone, and go off without a word. We are your friends, Frodo. Anyway: there it is. We know most of what Gandalf has told you. We know a good deal about the Ring. We are horribly afraid — but we are coming with you; or following you like hounds." [18]

---

[17] Tolkien, *The Return of the King* (New York: Ballantine Books), pp. 280-81.

[18] Ibid., p. 150.

But as time goes on they begin to reveal other qualities. Their cheerfulness persists in the face of danger and hardship; their frankness and friendliness win them the friendship of the formidable Treebeard. Merry's affection for King Théoden of the Rohirrim along with Pippin's quixotic offer of fealty to Denethor show a generosity only hinted at earlier. To some extent the various qualities which make us so fond of Bilbo in *The Hobbit* are distributed among the hobbits in the *Ring* trilogy, and Merry and Pippin have Bilbo's endearing perkiness and cheerfulness. Their very weaknesses make them more "human" — bring them nearer to us.

Gandalf can be a remote and enigmatic character, but his humor and his gruffness (a bark that is usually worse than his bite, at least for his friends) make him a memorable character and even one who inspires affection. Frodo composes his first poem when he believes Gandalf is dead. One of the lines is "swift in anger, quick to laugh," and even after Gandalf's apotheosis, his temper and his humor survive.

In a way, Gandalf is more "human" than Aragorn, more understandable and familiar to us than Gimli the dwarf of Legolas the elf. Gimli's astonished love for Galadriel humanizes him a bit. Legolas remains the most remote of the Fellowship, as Tolkien intends. But all three — Aragorn, Gimli, and Legolas — are intended by Tolkien to be somewhat remote. They are heroes or supermen. They do not lose their dignity, even when they momentarily lose their courage, as Legolas does at the sight of the Balrog and Gimli does on the Paths of the Dead.

It is not the heroes, but the very limited and fallible hobbits who are the real focus of the story. Perhaps Tolkien had learned from the early English poets that though Beowulf is a formidable character, the fallible Gawain is a more living one. Even Gandalf and Galadriel have the possibility of failing; they are both tempted by the power of the Ring, but are able to resist the temptation.

It may be well here to clear up a minor misunderstanding about the Ring itself. It has been blithely identified with Power by both friendly and unfriendly critics. Mary Ellman accused Tolkien's characters of being afraid of power, and even some of his admirers talk merely about the "dangers of power." But, of course, the Ring has not merely neutral power, but satanic power: the Dark Lord "has put a great part of his own power into it," and this is why its destruction does more than deprive Sauron of more power — it destroys him. When Gandalf and Galadriel refuse the Ring, it is not because "power corrupts"; they are, apart from Sauron, the most powerful persons in the story. Rather, they reject it because using the Ring to do good would be attempting to use Satan's power to do good, and this will inevitably defeat the good purpose and turn it to evil.

Saruman tries to tempt Gandalf with the power of the Ring and the plea that the end justifies the means.

" . . . listen, Gandalf, my old friend and helper!" he said, coming near and speaking now in a softer voice. "I said we, for we it may be, if you will join with me. A new Power is rising. Against it the old allies and policies will not avail us at all. There is no hope left in Elves or dying Numenor. This then is one choice before you, before us. We may join with that Power. It would be wise, Gandalf. There is hope that way. Its victory is at hand; and there will be rich reward for those that aided it. As the Power grows, its proved friends will also grow; and the Wise, such as you and I, may with patience come at last to direct its courses, to control it. We can bide our time, we can keep our thoughts in our hearts, deploring maybe evils done by the way, but approving the high and ultimate purpose: Knowledge, Rule, Order; all the

110

things that we have so far striven in vain to accomplish, hindered rather than helped by our weak or idle friends. There need not be, there would not be, any real change in our designs, only in our means." [19]

Both in the case of Saruman and in the case of Gollum, there is a sense that there may be a real possibility of their redemption. When Gandalf pleads with Saruman after his defeat, Saruman wavers for a moment. Just before Gollum betrays Frodo, he almost gives in to love for him. Each being in the story is good or evil by his own choice, and that choice is a genuinely free one, though powerful forces from inside and out attempt to influence it. As Gandalf says of Gollum:

"Even Gollum was not wholly ruined. He had proved tougher than even one of the Wise would have guessed — as a hobbit might. There was a little corner of his mind that was still his own, and light came through it, as through a chink in the dark: light out of the past. It was actually pleasant, I think, to hear a kindly voice again, bringing up memories of wind, and trees, and sun on the grass, and such forgotten things.

"But that, of course, would only make the evil part of him angrier in the end — unless it could be conquered. Unless it could be cured." Gandalf sighed "Alas! there is little hope of that for him. Yet not no hope. No, not though he possessed the Ring so long, almost as far back as he can remember. For it was long since he had worn it much: in the black darkness it was seldom needed. Certainly he had never 'faded.' He is thin and tough still. But the thing was eating up his mind, of course, and the torment had become almost unbearable." [20]

[19] Tolkien, *The Fellowship of the Ring*, p. 340.
[20] Ibid., pp. 86-87.

Remember the salient points we found in Lewis's discussion of good and evil, The responsibility of each person to do God's work, the danger of using evil means — this is Tolkien's message as well as Lewis's. The apparent absence of explicit religion in Tolkien will be discussed in the next chapter, but Tolkien's moral message seems to be the same as Lewis's.

The character of evil is also alike in Tolkien and Lewis. In Tolkien's stories, just as in Lewis's, one prominent characteristic of the evil characters is their inability to trust each other or cooperate with each other effectively. We get the first sketch of this in *The Hobbit*, where the first evil creatures encountered, the trolls, are defeated because of their quarreling with each other. At several crucial points in the *Ring* trilogy the hobbits are able to take advantage of the quarrels of orcs with other orcs (Merry and Pippin's escape from the Uruk-hai, Sam and Frodo's escape from Cirith Ungol). On a somewhat higher level, Saruman's rivalry with Sauron weakens both sides in the uneasy alliance, providing another advantage for the Fellowship of the Ring. And, as we have mentioned already, Sauron's inability to picture his adversaries as anything but rivals for his power is a key element in his final defeat. As Gandalf says before the last battle:

> Sauron knows . . . that the precious thing which he has lost has been found again . . . [and that] there are some among us with strength enough to wield it . . . it can be used only by one master alone, not by many; and he will look for a time of strife, ere one of the great among us makes himself master and puts down the others. . . . We must march out to meet him at once. We must make ourselves the bait. . . . He will take that bait, in hope and in greed, for he will think that in such rashness he sees the pride of a new Ringlord. [21]

---

[21] Tolkien, *The Return of the King*, p. 191.

And Gandalf says earlier,

> Let folly be our cloak, a veil before the eyes of the
> Enemy! For he is very wise, and weighs all things to a
> nicety in the scales of his malice. But the only meas-
> ure that he knows is desire, desire for power; and so
> he judges all hearts. Into his heart the thought will
> not enter that any will refuse it, that having the Ring
> we may seek to destroy it. If we seek this, we shall
> put him out of reckoning. [22]

The Fellowship of the Ring is, indeed, beyond Sauron's comprehension. The great hero and captain,
Aragorn, turns aside from his great destiny to become
the guide and protector of a young hobbit who has
hardly drawn a sword in anger. The elf, Legolas, and
the dwarf, Gimli, overcome the enmity of their races
and become fast friends. All three turn aside from
seemingly more important matters to pursue the Uruk-
hai day after day in hope of rescuing Merry and Pippin.
Even Boromir, nearly overcome by his desire for the
Ring, repents and dies sacrificing his life to save those
of the younger hobbits. Ironically, this is a "useless"
sacrifice, since the orcs have orders to take hobbits
alive. But it is Boromir's *amende honorable* and, we
are made to feel, his salvation. All of this loyalty,
sacrifice, subordination of higher to lower, would be
totally incomprehensible to Sauron, as Tolkien makes
us see.

In fact, as both Lewis and Tolkien show us, there
is a fatal contradiction on the side of evil. No one
in his right mind would want to be one of Sauron's
slaves. But one might, in certain moods, want to be
Sauron or, failing this, one of his satraps. Yet only
the highest throne is really secure; there is only one
position really worth having, even at the most cynical
estimate. Thus all but one on the side of darkness

---

[22] Tolkien, *The Fellowship of the Ring,* pp. 352-53.

are doomed to frustration. In the company of the good, however, there is a complicated "dance" of subordination; for example, Aragorn delights to honor Frodo and Frodo delights to honor him, and both delight to honor Sam. The mystery of evil is that it rejects joy for an ambition which is in its nature unattainable.

chapter 6

Religion in Tolkien

Many critics find no religious element at all in Tolkien's Middle-earth. But perhaps it is wise to make clear what we mean by the much-abused term "religion." I take it that the usual elements of religion are belief in a Being or Beings greater than man and worthy of worship, and a belief in some sort of life after death. Are these two elements present in Tolkien? There is a problem here for Tolkien, the Christian writing of a pre-Christian era, a problem which is illuminated by his comments on the Beowulf poet, who has essentially the same problem.

> He cast his time into the long-ago, because already the long-ago had a special poetical attraction. He knew much about old days and though his knowledge . . . was rich and poetical rather than accurate with the accuracy of modern archaeology (such as that is), one thing he knew clearly: those days were heathen — heathen, noble, and hopeless.

> But if the specifically Christian was suppressed, so also were the old gods. Partly because they had not really existed, and had been always, in the Christian view, only delusions or lies fabricated by the evil one, the *gastbona*, to whom the hopeless turned especially

115

in times of need. Partly because their old names (certainly not forgotten) had been potent, and were connected in memory still, not only with mythology or such fairy-tale matter as we find, say, in *Gylfaginning*, but with active heathendom, religion not actually essential to the theme.[1]

This is Tolkien's problem in a nutshell. If he shows his people at worship, for instance, who is he to show them worshiping? A man of Tolkien's activity of mind could invent fifty pantheons, with appropriate myths and rituals. But this would be to show his heroes worshiping false gods. Is he to make them monotheists then? But how is he to make their monotheism plausible? None of his races have a philosophical bent, like the Greeks. Is he to give them a special revelation, like the Hebrews? But if so, how is this to connect with the Judeo-Christian revelation? Wisely enough, Tolkien does not show his characters at worship.

And yet he does not entirely avoid the idea of superior beings, of worship. Hints here and there through the manuscript are expanded in the Appendices. There are the Valar, the "Guardians of the World," and behind them the figure of "the One." The Valar are not unlike more remote eldils, from the little we hear of them. But at one point this background religion comes into the foreground. If any group in Middle-earth is to be close to God or the gods, it should be the elves, and among these the High Elves.

For in Tolkien's imaginary history the High Elves are those who have dwelt in the Blessed Realm, the Undying Lands, and have then returned to Middle-earth to live for a while before returning via the Grey

[1] "Beowulf: the Monsters and the Critics" in *An Anthology of Beowulf Criticism,* ed. Lewis E. Nicholson (Notre Dame, Ind.: University of Notre Dame Press, 1963), pp. 71-72.

Havens. They are the wisest, best, and most powerful of all the races in Middle-earth, and all of the greatest Elf-figures in legend and song, as well as in the main story, are of the High-elven kindred.

Now look at the early part of Frodo's adventures, when he has left Bag End, but not yet the Shire. He and his companions fall in with a group of elves, who are singing this song:

> Snow-white! Snow-white! O Lady clear!
>   O Queen beyond the Western Seas!
> O Light to us that wander here
>   Amid the world of woven trees!
>
> Gilthoniel! A Elbereth!
>   Clear are thy eyes and bright thy breath,
> Snow-white! Snow-white! We sing to thee
>   In a far land beyond the Sea.
>
> O stars that in the Sunless Year
>   With shining hands by her were sown
> In windy fields now bright and clear
>   We see your silver blossom blown!
>
> O Elbereth! Gilthoniel!
>   We still remember, we who dwell
> In this far land beneath the trees,
>   Thy starlight on the Western Seas.

The song ended. "These are High-Elves! They spoke the name of Elbereth!" said Frodo in amazement."[2]

Elbereth is "Queen beyond the Western Seas"; we shall explore the significance of this in a moment. But if the "stars . . . with shining hands by her were sown," she is evidently something like a goddess, even if the language is partly metaphorical. "O Light to us that wander here" recalls certain Roman Catholic hymns to the Blessed Virgin. And indeed, Elbereth seems

---

[2] Tolkien, *The Fellowship of the Ring,* rev. ed. (New York: Ballantine Books, 1969), p. 117.

to play a part very similar to that of Mary in Catholic worship.

Later on, when the Fellowship of the Ring are leaving Lothlórien, the great Elf-queen Galadriel sings a song. It is given in "Elvish" with a translation attached.

"Ah! like gold fall the leaves in the wind, long years numberless as the wings of trees! The long years have passed like swift draughts of the sweet mead in lofty halls beyond the West beneath the blue vaults of Varda wherein the stars tremble in the song of her voice, holy and queenly. Who now shall refill the cup for me? For now the Kindler, Varda, the Queen of the Stars, from Mount everwhite has uplifted her hands like clouds, and all paths are drowned deep in shadow; and out of a grey country darkness lies on the foaming waves between us, and mist covers the jewels of Calacirya for ever. Now lost, lost to those from the East is Valimar! Farewell! Maybe thou shalt find Valimar. Maybe even thou shalt find it. Farewell!" Varda is the name of that Lady whom the Elves in these lands of exile name Elbereth. [3]

Here again, the terms used of Varda are appropriate only to a goddess or a saint. Gildor also says to the hobbits, "May Elbereth protect you" (p. 124), which makes sense only if Elbereth is supposed to have the power to know what is happening to the companions and power to help them. Such expressions as "May God protect you," "May Mary protect you," "May St. Patrick protect you" make sense, but if we substitute merely historical or legendary figures we get nonsense: "May George Washington protect you," "May Uncle Sam protect you."

Elbereth is invoked by the hobbits at every moment of crisis — for instance, at the first attack of the Black Riders, when Frodo puts himself in great peril by

---

[3] Ibid., p. 489.

putting on the ring. "The third figure . . . sprang forward and bore down on Frodo. At that moment Frodo threw himself forward on the ground, and he heard himself crying aloud: 'O Elbereth! Gilthoniel!' At the same time he struck at the feet of his enemy." [4] He calls on Elbereth again at the Ringwraiths' next attack (p. 286). Again, when Sam rescues Frodo from the tower of Cirith Ungol, he must leave him to hunt for disguises for them: "Now you draw up the ladder, if you can Mr. Frodo, and don't you let it down till you hear me call the pass-word. *Elbereth* I'll call. What the Elves say. No orc would say that." [5] Just before this, Sam, in his fight with Shelob, has called on Elbereth.

In fact, as we look through the whole trilogy, with our minds alerted to the importance of Elbereth's name, we are surprised at the number of times it is mentioned. At many moments of crisis there is some mention of invocation of Elbereth, especially by the elves (Gildor, Galadriel), but also by Sam and Frodo. Men and dwarves do not call on her, nor does Gandalf, although he mentions her name with respect. It seems that Elbereth is primarily the Lady of the Elves and secondarily the patroness or protector of Elf-friends like Sam and Frodo. By them she is invoked in danger, and songs are sung in her praise. This is far from any formal worship, of course, but we have found a bright being invoked by the highest race of creatures — as we might expect — and called on by the heroes of the story at the moments of greatest crisis — as we might expect.

Outside of the trilogy itself there is one more source of information — the notes, mainly linguistic, that Tolkien contributed to *The Road Goes Ever On*, a song

[4] Ibid., p. 263.
[5] Tolkien, *The Return of the King* (New York: Ballantine Books), p. 231.

cycle based on Tolkien's poetry with music by Donald Swann. In discussing the elvish words of the song "A Elbereth Gilthoniel," mentioned above, Tolkien draws a parallel with Sam's invocation of Elbereth before his battle with Shelob. Amid the linguistic details, he makes this point in passing:

> As a "divine" or "angelic" person Varda/Elbereth could be said to be "looking afar from heaven" (as in Sam's invocation); hence the use of a present participle. She was often thought of, or depicted, as standing on a great height looking towards Middle-earth, with eyes that penetrated the shadows, and listening for the cries for aid of Elves (and Men) in peril or grief. Frodo (Vol. I, p. 208) and Sam both invoke her in moments of extreme peril. The Elves sing hymns to her. (These and other references to religion in *The Lord of the Rings* are frequently overlooked.) [6]

This comment in passing by Tolkien seems to confirm all that we have guessed from the trilogy itself. Elbereth is "divine" or "angelic"; the songs the elves sing to her are called specifically "'hymns." She can hear and answer "cries for aid." She hears the cries primarily of elves, and men are mentioned parenthetically as also crying to her.

I think this is the clearest statement that Tolkien has given about religion in the *Ring* trilogy, and characteristically it is an oblique reference in a series of remarks on elvish philology.

In view of the difficulties we have considered above, these hints are perhaps all Tolkien can be expected to give us. I think, by the way, that there are elements of personality and personal history involved in Tolkien's failure to say much about God. Tolkien was a more reticent man than Lewis, by all accounts, and

[6] Donald Swann and J. R. R. Tolkien, *The Road Goes Ever On: A Song Cycle* (New York: Ballantine Books), p. 65.

less inclined to speak much of the things closest to his heart. Also, Tolkien, practically a cradle-Catholic, was less inclined to talk about religion than Lewis, the convert to Christianity.

About life after death there is an interesting situation in Tolkien's world. The elves are immortal and, when they leave Middle-earth, go to live "beyond the Western Seas in Elvenhome or Eressëa. This is a place to which one can physically voyage and yet also somehow otherworldly: "in Eressëa, in Elvenhome that no man can discover" (Return, p. 289). It is not the same as the Uttermost West: "the seed of that tree before came from Eressëa, and before that out of the Uttermost West" (Fellowship, p. 321). Numenor, Tolkien's version of Atlantis, was "the westernmost of all mortal lands . . . [from it] the farsighted could see the white tower of the Haven of the Eldar in Eressëa" (Return, p. 390). Later in the same paragraph:

> But one command had been laid upon the Numenoreans, the "Ban of the Valar"; they were forbidden to sail west out of sight of their own shores or attempt to set foot on the Undying Lands. For though a long span of life had been granted them [the Numenoreans] . . . they must remain mortal, since the Valar were not permitted to take from them the Gift of Men (or the Doom of Men, as it was afterwards called). [7]

When they break this prohibition and "set foot on the shores of Aman the Blessed, the valar laid down their Guardianship, and called upon the One, and the world was changed. Numenor was thrown down and swallowed in the sea, and the Undying Lands were removed for ever from the circles of the world." [8]

Here we have the elements of the background re-

---

[7] Tolkien, *The Return of the King,* p. 390.
[8] Ibid., p. 392.

ligion we mentioned before: the valar, who like eldils give orders to mortals and punish the breaking of their rules; the One behind the valar. (Elbereth, one presumes, is one of the valar.) Eressëa is evidently an earthly paradise, where all who dwell have unending life. Unending but not, I think, eternal. There is a suggestion that at the end of this world Eressëa, too, will end, and the elves go on to some heavenly destiny. Meanwhile, they live in Eressëa.

We can reconstruct the geography of Tolkien's imagined world in this fashion. The Uttermost West is the dwelling of the godlike valar, who give commands to men and even to elves, although these commands are not always obeyed. East of the Uttermost West is Eressëa, the dwelling-place of the elves. East of this was "the great Isle of Elenna, westernmost of all Mortal lands [where] they founded the realm of Numenor" (*Return*, p. 390). But Elenna has sunk into the sea, leaving no land, apparently, between Middle-earth and Eressëa. Does all this imply a flat earth? Numenor sank into the sea and eventually "the Undying Lands were removed for ever from the circles of the world." Thus, even if Middle-earth is identified with Europe, the fact that one can sail west from Europe without encountering either Atlantis or the Blessed Realm does not contradict Tolkien's imagined history.

Of course, the idea that gods or angels could have a local habitation, a literal "land" or "realm" and not a metaphorical one, is strange to modern minds. But it fits very well into the mythical atmosphere of Tolkien's world.

Nor does this imaginary history necessarily contradict Tolkien's Christianity. That human beings once shared the earth with other rational beings, that they were all under the rule and guardianship of some sort of supernatural being, that they faced the servants of the Evil One in physical battles — none of this contradicts anything in Christian belief, any more than the similar situation on Lewis's Malacandra does.

The wizards or *istari*, such as Gandalf and Saruman, may indeed be physical manifestations or embodiments of the mysterious valar. They are described as follows:

> When maybe a thousand years had passed, and the first shadow had fallen on Greenwood the Great, the *Istari* or Wizards appeared in Middle-earth. It was afterwards said that they came out of the Far West and were messengers sent to contest the power of Sauron, and to unite all those who had the will to resist him; but they were forbidden to match his power with power, or to seek to dominate Elves or Men by force and fear.

> They came therefore in the shape of Men, though they were never young and aged only slowly, and they had many powers of mind and hand. They revealed their true names to few, but used such names as were given to them. The two highest of this order (of whom it is said there were five) were called by the Eldar Curunir, "the Man of Skill," and Mithrandir, "the Grey Pilgrim," but by Men in the North Saruman and Gandalf. Curunir journeyed often into the East, but dwelt at last in Isengard. Mithrandir was closest in friendship with the Eldar, and wandered mostly in the West, and never made for himself any lasting abode. [9]

"In the shape of Men" does not necessarily mean "not men," but it hints at it.

In response to a question, Tolkien has said that Gandalf is "an angel." [10] Using the terms of Tolkien's own mythology, this suggests that Gandalf is one of the valar, the Guardians. Is this true of all wizards?

---

[9] Ibid., p. 455.

[10] Neil D. Isaacs and Rose A. Zimbardo, eds., *Tolkien and the Critics* (Notre Dame, Ind.: University of Notre Dame Press, 1968), p. 35.

Then Saruman is similarly one of the "angels," but a fallen one. Perhaps even Sauron and his more remote predecessor in evil, Morgoth the Enemy (*Return*, p. 388), are Guardians who have betrayed their guardianship.

Again the notes to *The Road Goes Ever On* give us some help. In explaining an Elvish word which means "veil," Tolkien remarks that

> The simple word *fana* acquired a special sense. Owing to the close association of the High-Elves with the Valar it was applied to the "veils" or "raiment" in which the Valar presented themselves to physical eyes. These were the bodies in which they were self-incarnated. They usually took the shape of the bodies of Elves (and Men). The Valar assumed these forms when, after their demiurgic labours they came and dwelt in Arda, "the realm." They did so because of their love and desire for the Children of God (*Erusēn*), for whom they were to prepare the "realm." The future forms of elves and men had been revealed to them, though they had no part in their design or making, and the precise time of their appearance was not known. In these *fanar* they later presented themselves to the Elves (though they could also assume other wholly "inhuman" shapes, which were seldom seen by Elves or Men). [They] appeared as persons of majestic (not gigantic) stature, vested in robes expressing their individual natures and functions. The High-Elves said that these forms were always to some degree radiant, as if suffused with a light from within. [11]

This links up with our previous speculations and suggests others. Is even the Balrog, for example, perhaps a fallen valar, imprisoned in "inhuman" form? Gandalf speaks to it as if they shared some secret knowledge: "You cannot pass," he said. . . . "I am

---

[11] Swann and Tolkien, *The Road Goes Ever On*, p. 66.

a servant of the Secret Fire, wielder of the flame of Anor. You cannot pass. The dark fire will not avail you, dark flame of Udûn. Go back to the Shadow!" (*Fellowship*, p. 429). And if the Balrog is not a being of the same degree of power as Gandalf, how can it nearly destroy him?

Gandalf is described as dying and coming to life again. In the Chronology of Appendix B we have the entries:

> January 23 Gandalf pursues the Balrog to the peak of Zirak-Zigil.
>
> January 25 He casts down the Balrog and passes away. His body lies on the peak.
>
> February 14 . . . Gandalf returns to life. . . . [12]

At his first reappearance to his friends Gandalf is almost transfigured.

> He laid his hand on Gimli's head, and the Dwarf looked up and laughed suddenly. "Gandalf!" he said. "But you are all in white!"
>
> "Yes, I am in white now," said Gandalf. "Indeed I am Saruman, one might almost say, Saruman as he should have been. But come now, tell me of yourselves! I have passed through fire and deep water, since we parted. I have forgotten much that I thought I knew, and learned again much that I had forgotten. I can see many things far off, but many things that are close at hand I cannot see. Tell me of yourselves!" [13]

This suggests that the fight with the Balrog has destroyed Gandalf's connection with the *fana*, the physical envelope in which he is "self-incarnate," and

---

[12] Tolkien, *The Return of the King,* p. 465.

[13] Tolkien, *The Two Towers*, rev. ed. (New York: Ballantine Books, 1969), pp. 124-25.

he must restore his connection with it, thereby giving his *fana* new attributes. Perhaps in the interim he returned to some form of noncorporal life. Then he is recognized by his companions: "Gandalf," the old man repeated, as if recalling from old memory a long disused word. "Yes, that was the name. I was Gandalf" (*Two Towers*, p. 124). His "body" has apparently lain on Zirak-Zigil for three weeks (January 25 to February 14); I am not sure of the significance of this, though the three weeks perhaps remind us of the three days during which Christ was in the tomb.

It is interesting to compare Tolkien's "angelology" with Lewis's. The statement that angelic beings can assume either human or inhuman forms suggests the scene in *Perelandra* where the eldils assume human forms to honor the King and the Green Lady, after experimenting with various inhuman manifestations. The fact that the Oyarses of Perelandra and Malacandra are "feminine (not female)" and "masculine (not male)" suggest the genders of Tolkien's valar. Elbereth is said to be in some sense the "spouse" of Manwe, the Elder King, chief of the valar (*The Road Goes Ever On*, p. 66). The "demiurgic work" of the valar reminds us of Lewis's use of the Neoplatonic idea of angels as the "ruling Intelligences" of heavenly bodies. But it is made quite clear that angels do not "design or make" the forms of men or elves. Both Lewis and Tolkien believe angels are real beings, but their fictional angels borrow details from philosophical speculation and from myth.

The parallels between Gandalf's "resurrection" and that of Christ are obvious, so obvious it may be worthwhile to say something again about Tolkien's attitude toward allegory. In the introduction to the Ballantine edition of the trilogy he says,

As for any inner meaning or "message," it has in the intention of the author none. It is neither allegorical nor topical. . . . I cordially dislike allegory in all its manifestations, and always have done so since I grew old and wary enough to detect its presence. I much prefer history, true or feigned, with its varied applicability to the thought and experience of readers. I think that many confuse "applicability" with "allegory"; but the one resides in the freedom of the reader, and the other in the purposed domination of the author.

An author cannot of course remain wholly unaffected by his experience, but the ways in which a story-germ uses the soil of experience are extremely complex, and attempts to define the process are at best guesses from evidence that is inadequate and ambiguous. [14]

Thus Tolkien, by his own account, is not writing what we called strict allegory. Nor, I contend, is he writing what I have called "loose allegory"; he is not attempting to tell us that "life is like this." Rather, he is telling us a story, which can be enjoyed purely in its own right. Like all good stories, it has echoes of others, including that greatest of all stories — which Tolkien believes is a true story — the life of Christ.

Gandalf and Frodo are not allegorical masks for Christ, as in a strict allegory, nor symbols for some aspect of human condition, as in a loose allegory. They are people in their own right. But because they are almost real people they can, as real people can, express Christ in their own way.

It is part of the Roman Catholic idea of the saints that each mirrors Christ in an individual way, expressing facets of the infinite Personality which could not all be expressed in one finite life, no matter how great. The historical Christ, for example, was not a philosopher, nor a king; but St. Thomas Aquinas and St.

---

[14] *The Fellowship of the Ring,* p. x-xi.

Louis of France show us something of what He might have been like if He had been. Thus Gandalf and Frodo, while being very real and very individual, also have something to tell us about Christ.

In this Tolkien is, I might say, contrasted with Lewis as Catholic to Protestant. In Lewis there are Maleldil and the eldils, and there is Aslan in the Narnia stories. But in Lewis's Protestant Christian imagination there is no human or quasi-human mediator between God and man. On the other hand, in Tolkien's Catholic Christian imagination we have Elbereth, whom it would not surprise us to find addressed as "Our Lady," and we have elves and wizards who are like the wonderworking saints of medieval legend. In Frodo we see the imitation of Christ on a more human level.

Both tendencies, in fiction and also in real life, have their dangers. Lewis says, in *The Allegory of Love,*

> When Catholicism goes bad it becomes the world-old, world-wide *religio* of amulets and holy places and priestcraft: Protestantism, in its corresponding decay, becomes a vague mist of ethical platitudes. Catholicism is accused of being much too like all the other religions; Protestantism of being insufficiently like a religion at all. Hence Plato, with his transcendent Forms, is the doctor of Protestants; Aristotle, with his immanent Forms, the doctor of Catholics. [15]

In fiction Tolkien's "saints" are in some danger of degenerating into "superman" figures, and the closeness of our confrontation with Aslan and Maleldil in Lewis is sometimes almost embarrassing. But both men avoid the dangers, by and large. Gandalf, even after his apotheosis, does not become all-powerful: he

---

[15] *The Allegory of Love* (New York: Oxford University Press, 1925), p. 323.

is still in danger from the Black Riders. And Aslan the lion can say and do things which in a human figure would be embarrassing. Again, the eldils contrast with and highlight the impression we get of Maleldil. The elves, though good and powerful, are not perfect any more than Gandalf is. They are not really very interested in humans or hobbits — they go their own way.

> The Elves have their own labours and their own sorrows, and they are little concerned with the ways of hobbits, or of any other creatures upon earth. Our paths cross theirs seldom, by chance or purpose. In this meeting there may be more than chance; but the purpose is not clear to me, and I fear to say too much. [16]

Also, they are limited in at least some ways: For instance, they can be killed, in battle or by accident. Tolkien never quite says what happens then; perhaps they simply appear in Eressëa.

In the story of Aragorn and his Elf-bride Arwen — which is told in an appendix — Arwen, who chooses to live and die as a mortal to share the fate of her husband, is described as the only elf to truly die. Since great numbers of elves are apparently slain in various battles in The Hobbit and the Ring trilogy, this would seem to imply that these somehow did not really die. Some sort of translation "beyond the Western Sea" for elves who "die" in Middle-earth would account for this apparent inconsistency. Certainly the elves have no fear of death; and when Legolas goes with Aragorn on the Paths of the Dead "there was not a heart among them that did not quail, unless it were the heart of Legolas of the Elves, for whom the ghosts of Men have no terror" (Return, p. 70). At the attack on the Fellowship at the ford near Rivendell, Frodo sees Glorfindel the Elf-prince as a shining white figure.

---

[16] Tolkien, *The Fellowship of the Ring,* pp. 123-24.

Gandalf tells him later, "You saw him for a moment as he is upon the other side" (*Fellowship*, p. 294). Evidently the elves are not wholly of this world even when they dwell in Middle-earth.

What of hobbits? As far as I can see, Tolkien gives no answer at all to this except in the cases of Frodo and Sam, both of whom join the elves in their earthly paradise as a reward for their struggles. There is some suggestion of a sort of limbo for dwarves in *The Hobbit*; when Thorin is dying he says, "I go now to the halls of waiting to sit beside my fathers, until the world is renewed" (*Hobbit*, p. 272).

In Catholic theological speculation, the good men who lived before the time of Christ wait in "the Limbo of the Fathers" for the redemptive death of Christ, after which they may enter heaven. Nothing Tolkien says either suggests or denies that this is the case, except some hints in the case of the marriages between men and Elf-maids. By choosing to marry Aragorn, Arwen is evidently to choose the lot of a mortal and *thus* to be separated from her elvish kindred — "a bitter parting beyond the end of the world" (*Return*, p. 423).

Thus we have the following situation: the fate of elves is immortality in Eressëa; the fate of dwarves to "go to the halls of waiting . . . until the world is renewed"; and the fate of men and hobbits is left uncertain except that death is called "the gift of the One to Men" (*Return*, p. 428).

So much for *explicitly* religious elements. But the whole framework of the *Ring* trilogy is that of a struggle between good and evil on a cosmic scale, with everyone having to choose one side or another. Furthermore, there is a plan behind what happens; Frodo was *meant* to find the Ring (*Fellowship*, p. 65).

As Patricia Meyer Spacks says in an essay collected in the Isaacs and Zimbardo volume:

A theological scheme is implied though not directly stated in *The Lord of the Rings*, and it is of primary importance to the work. The fact of freedom of the will implies a structured universe, a universe like the Christian one in that only through submission to the Good can true freedom be attained — willing acceptance of evil involves necessary loss of freedom; a universe like the Christian one, further, in that it includes the possibility of Grace. . . . If the trilogy as has been said deals with a pre-religious age, an age in which worship was confined to adherence to a special ethos, the fact remains that the author includes in it all the necessary materials for religion. [17]

A little of Tolkien's feelings about religion comes out in one of his short pieces, "Leaf by Niggle" (reprinted in *The Tolkien Reader*), the nearest thing to allegory that Tolkien has written.

There was once a little man called Niggle, who had a long journey to make. He did not want to go, indeed the whole idea was distasteful to him; but he could not get out of it. He knew he would have to start some time, but he did not hurry with his preparations. [18]

The first stage in the journey is a "hospital" where Niggle works hard and lives a restricted life. He then goes on to a country place that is like the landscape of a great picture that Niggle, a painter, had been working on before his journey. Finally he travels on "to walk ever further and further towards the Mountains, always up hill" (p. 109).

The journey, of course, is death; the preparations, those preparations for death that we all neglect. The period of treatment that Niggle undergoes at the "hos-

[17] Isaacs and Zimbardo, eds., *Tolkien and the Critics*, pp. 86, 89-90.
[18] *Tree and Leaf* in *The Tolkien Reader* (New York: Ballantine Books, 1966), p. 85.

pital" is something like the Catholic idea of purgatory; the journey into the Mountains is "exploration into God" (in Christopher Fry's fine phrase). But there are some very idiosyncratic elements in this afterlife as pictured by Tolkien. First, part of the effect of the "hospital treatment" on Niggle is a seemingly prosaic change.

> He could take up a task the moment one bell rang, and lay it aside promptly the moment the next one went, all tidy and ready to be continued at the right time. He got through quite a lot in a day, now; he finished small things neatly. He had no "time of his own" (except alone in his bed-cell), and yet he was becoming master of his time; he began to know just what he could do with it. There was no sense of rush. He was quieter inside now, and at resting-time he could really rest. [19]

But it is this change that enables him to finish the work of art which he had left unfinished on earth. In doing this he has the help of Parish, whom he had somewhat grudgingly helped when both were alive. Only after completing this work can he go on to the Mountains.

One critic has suggested that "Leaf by Niggle" was written at ta period when Tolkien had despaired of finishing the Ring trilogy. Niggle's unfinished picture may then be a symbol of Tolkien's unfinished work. (The interruptions of the work required by charity and duty would then give some hint of why that work was so long unfinished.) But after completion of the "picture" and Niggle's departure, the "picture" — really now a sort of little sub-world — is used as a sort of preparation area for others who are learning to be strong enough to journey on into the Mountains. "'It is proving very useful indeed," said the Second

---

[19] Ibid., p. 98.

Voice. 'As a holiday, and a refreshment. It is splendid for convalescence; and not only for that, for many it is the best introduction to the Mountains. It works wonders in some cases. I am sending more and more there. They seldom have to come back.'" [20] This, I think, gives a very good idea of how Tolkien sees his work, "rest and refreshment," "convalescence" from the modern view of the world but also "for many . . . the best introduction to the Mountains." But since an introduction is not the thing itself, we also see perhaps why the religious element in the Ring trilogy, while present, is muted and in the background.

[20] Ibid., p. 112.

chapter 7

Religion in Lewis

In view of many misunderstandings, perhaps the first thing to notice about religion in Lewis's imaginative works is that there is much less of it than some people seem to suppose.

When we remember that the Roses call Lewis's space trilogy "a formal apology for Christianity," it comes as something of a shock to find that of the 160 pages of *Silent Planet* in the paperback edition, only 27 contain anything which might be called a religious reference. The first four or five are casual indications that Ransom is a believer; he contemplates suicide and, since he is "a pious man," hopes he will be forgiven if forced to it. At the landing of the spaceship he "licked his dry lips and prayed for the end"; when he hopes to escape, "he prayed and felt his knife." Waking after his first night on Mars, "he applied himself vigorously to his devotions and his toilet." There is a mention of "Paradise" when he finds the "talking beast," his first Martian. (You will see I am trying to count all possible references.) He finds that the Martians are monotheists, who use the name Maleldil for God. After this there are a dozen or so references to Maleldil in connection with crops, the way man is constituted, death, and so on. When Ransom meets the eldils, the evil ruling eldil of our world is more or less identified with Satan, and the Oyarsa of Mars evinces curiosity about God's dealings with Earth including, presumably, the Incarnation. (Earth is "blockaded," and no direct information reaches the eldils.) In the concluding chapter it is said that the dangers represented by the forces behind Weston are "not temporal, but eternal." Some of these references are important to the plot; none are vital. It would be possible, in fact, to remove all of these references without destroying the story or perhaps without even seriously damaging it. But the point is that these scattered references, important to the plot or not, are seen by the Roses as "a formal apology for Christianity."

There are two reasons for this, I think. One is that the Roses expect to find Lewis an "allegorical" writer and therefore find allegory where it is not really present as, for example, in the different occupations of the three Martian races. The second, the question of "hierarchy," we have already discussed. The Martians and Ransom agree that man should obey God. The Martians also assume that rational animals will be subject to eldils — which, as we have seen, is not true on Earth or Venus.

But Lewis did not write strict or even loose allegory, except for his early work, The Pilgrim's Regress. All of his stories rest on what may be called a "supposal" or, as Lewis sometimes called it, a "feigning." Suppose (or feign) that a man reached another planet and found unfallen races. . . . suppose that the story of the fall of man were played out again on a different world, but this time we feign a man of our own world is present. . . . suppose there is another world, of talking beasts and dwarves and fauns, and in that world we feign Christ is a great lion, the king of the beasts.

The story often consists of supposing or feigning these things and *then* going on to explore the consequences of this supposal. As Lewis says in a letter:

> By an allegory I mean a composition (whether pictorial or literary) in which immaterial realities are represented by feigned physical objects; e.g. a pictured Cupid allegorically represents erotic love (which in reality is an experience, not an object occupying a given area of space) or, in Bunyan, a giant represents Despair.

> If Aslan represented the immaterial Deity in the same way in which Giant Despair represents Despair, he would be an allegorical figure. In reality however he is an invention giving an imaginary answer to the question, "What might Christ become like, if there really were a world like Narnia and He chose to be incarnate and die and rise again in *that* world as He actually has done in ours?" This is not allegory at all. So in *Perelandra*. This also works out a *supposition*. ("Suppose, even now, in some other planet there were a first couple undergoing the same that Adam and Eve underwent here, but successfully.")

> Allegory and such supposals differ because they mix the real and the unreal in different ways. Bunyan's picture of Giant Despair does not start from supposal at all. It is not a supposition but a *fact* that despair can capture and imprison a human soul. What is unreal (fictional) is the giant, the castle, and the dungeon. The Incarnation of Christ in another world is mere supposal; but *granted* the supposition, He would really have been a physical object in that world as He was in Palestine and His death on the Stone Table would have been a physical event no less than his death on Calvary. Similarly, if the angels (who I believe to be real beings in the actual universe) have that relation to the Pagan gods which they are assumed to have in Perelandra, they might *really* manifest themselves in real form as they did to Ransom. Again, Ransom (to some extent) plays the role of Christ not because he allegorically repre-

sents Him (as Cupid represents falling in love) but because in reality every real Christian is really called upon in some measure to *enact* Christ. Of course Ransom does this rather more spectacularly than most. But that does not mean that he does it allegorically. It only means that fiction (at any rate my kind of fiction) chooses extreme cases. [1]

Note that what Lewis is doing is not like most illustrative fantasy, where the real interest is in certain aspects of human nature or the human condition, which are merely isolated and exaggerated by the supposal. Rather, Lewis is interested in these supposals partly for their own sake and partly because they provide a restatement in new terms of ideas which Lewis held to be true on other grounds. The restatement in terms of fantasy enables us to see them with fresh eyes — remember Tolkien's idea of Recovery — but is also interesting in itself. To take a not-altogether-fanciful parallel, a young man in love might try to imagine his beloved as she might have been if she had been born in another age or in another world. These imaginings might help him understand her better or appreciate her more, but it might also simply be a way of delighting in her "infinite variety."

Lewis was, I think, genuinely enamored of certain basic Christian ideas. He stated them clearly and gracefully in his radio talks, which have been collected in *Mere Christianity*, [2] and defended them in his various apologetic works. But those who think Lewis intended his fictional works as *arguments* for Christianity obviously have little idea of what argument is. Lewis did, and he gave very good arguments when it was his business to argue. Of course, one may

[1] W. H. Lewis, ed., *Letters of C. S. Lewis* (New York: Harcourt, Brace & World, 1965), p. 283.
[2] New York: The Macmillan Co., 1943.

propagandize for a view in literature in a variety of ways, but the attempt to rule out any attempt in literature to create sympathy or understanding for a given view would rule out at least half of admittedly great literature.

Just as the explicitly theological elements in *Silent Planet* may in theory be left out without destroying the story, so *That Hideous Strength* may be read purely as a thrilling combat between good and evil forces — without adverting to the fact that the evil forces are quite literally diabolical, the powerful beings on the side of good literally angels, and the good side literally God's side. The reader of science fiction will remember many stories of conflict almost equally cosmic.

Perelandra is more explicitly theological, for the framework of the story is the temptation of a new Eve and a possible, and only barely averted, new Fall — not of man but of the manlike race inhabiting Venus. Thus it has certain resemblances to *Paradise Lost* and, indeed, the parallels are interesting ones. In Milton's work Satan is in many ways the chief character. Lewis, among others, has argued against the often-encountered idea that Milton's Satan is intended to be a sympathetic character, or that he succeeds in any way in being an admirable or heroic character. Be this as it may, Lewis's Tempter in *Perelandra* avoids any possibility of admiration by any sane mind, or at least so one would think. It is one of the most chilling representations of sheer evil in literature. Here is the description of Ransom's reaction when he realized that the body of Weston had become a mere vehicle for Satan or one of his cohorts:

> And now, forcing its way up into consciousness, thrusting aside every mental habit and every longing not to believe, came the conviction that this, in fact, was not a man: that Weston's body was kept, walking and undecaying, in Perelandra by some wholly

different kind of life, and that Weston himself was gone.

It looked at Ransom in silence and at last began to smile. We have all often spoken — Ransom himself had often spoken — of a devilish smile. Now he realizes that he had never taken the words seriously. The smile was not bitter, nor raging, nor, in an ordinary sense, sinister; it was not even mocking. It seemed to summon Ransom, with horrible naiveté of welcome, into the world of its own pleasures, as if all men were at one in those pleasures, as if they were the most natural thing in the world and no dispute could ever have occurred about them. It was not furtive, nor ashamed, it had nothing of the conspirator in it. It did not defy goodness, it ignored it to the point of annihilation. Ransom perceived that he had never before seen anything but half-hearted and uneasy attempts at evil. This creature was whole-hearted. The extremity of its evil had passed beyond all struggle into some state which bore a horrible similarity to innocence. It was beyond vice as the Lady was beyond virtue.[3]

The sight of the Unman's face is so terrible that Ransom faints. When he comes to himself he remembers an old belief that the mere sight of the devil was one of the greatest torments of hell. The Unman does not again show himself as so terrible, but we see him tormenting Ransom and torturing some of the Perelandran animals.

Terrible as the Unman is, he is also clearly seen as despicable.

No imagined horror could have surpassed the sense which grew within him as the slow hours passed, that this creature was, by all human standards, inside out — its heart on the surface and its shallowness at the heart. On the surface, great designs and an

3 C. S. Lewis, *Perelandra* (New York: The Macmillan Co., n.d.), pp. 110-11.

antagonism to Heaven which involved the fate of worlds: but deep within, when every veil had been pierced, was there, after all, nothing but a black puerility, an aimless empty spitefulness content to state itself with the tiniest cruelties, as love does not disdain the smallest kindness? [4]

Eventually Ransom must fight physically with the Unman to prevent him from wearing down the Green Lady's resistance by "third-degree" tactics. Ransom's reactions during the fight vary from terror to pity to what one might almost call "holy hatred."

An experience that perhaps no good man can ever have in our world came over him — a torrent of perfectly unmixed and lawful hatred. The energy of hating, never before felt without some guilt, without some dim knowledge that he was failing fully to distinguish the sinner from the sin, rose into his arms and legs till he felt that they were pillars of burning blood. What was before him appeared no longer a creature of corrupted will. It was corruption itself to which will was attached only as an instrument. Ages ago it had been a Person: but the ruins of personality now survived in it only as weapons at the disposal of a furious self-exiled negation. [5]

There are interesting parallels here to Tolkien's elves, who seem to have a similar complete aversion to the orcs and their master, the Dark Lord. Even the name of the orcs in elvish speech is *yrch*, which sounds almost like a gagging or spitting sound.

The Perelandran Eve, the Green Lady, may be compared in various ways with Galadriel and the other feminine figures in the *Ring* trilogy. She is less remote and mysterious than they, but she is undoubtedly a great lady, though as the first woman of her race she is naive and childish in some ways. In fact, Lewis

[4] Ibid., p. 123.
[5] Ibid., pp. 155-56.

assumed an extraordinarily difficult task in attempting to draw such a character. He discussed some of the problems in a letter to a friend who was one of the group of Anglican nuns to whom Perelandra is dedicated.

9 November 1941

I've got Ransom to Venus and through his first conversation with the "Eve" of that world: a difficult chapter. I hadn't realized till I came to write it all the Ave-Eva business. I may have embarked on the impossible. This woman has got to combine characteristics which the Fall has put poles apart — she's got to be some ways like a Pagan goddess and in other ways like the Blessed Virgin. But if one can get even a fraction of it into words, it is worth doing. [6]

It is interesting to compare Lewis's story of an averted Fall with his comments on Milton's Paradise Lost. Part of Lewis's aim in his Preface to Paradise Lost is to defend Milton against charges that he departed from Christian orthodoxy and introduced theological novelties of his own in the Fall story. In reply to this, Lewis argues that "Milton's version of the Fall story is substantially that of St. Augustine, which is that of the Church as a whole." [7] The following summary of this version (paraphrased from Lewis's account) casts interesting light on the Perelandra story:

God created all things good; what we call bad things are good things perverted. Good can exist without evil, but not evil without good. Though God has made all creatures good He knows that some will voluntarily make themselves bad, and He also knows the good use which He will then make of their badness. Who-

[6] W. H. Lewis, ed., Letters of C. S. Lewis, p. 195.

[7] A Preface to Paradise Lost (New York: Oxford University Press, 1942), p. 66.

ever tries to rebel against God produces the result opposite to His intention. Those who will not become God's sons become His tools. If there had been no Fall, the human race after multiplying to its full numbers would have been elevated to angelic status. The Fall consisted in disobedience. The apple was not bad or harmful except insofar as it was forbidden, and the only point of forbidding it was to instill obedience. While the Fall *consisted in* disobedience, it *resulted* from pride. Hence Satan approaches Eve through her pride: first by flattery and second by urging her selfhood to direct revolt against being subject at all. Finally, the great moral of the story of the Fall is "that Obedience to the will of God makes men happy and that Disobedience makes them miserable" (see pp. 66-71 of *Preface*).

In Perelandra Lewis uses this full battery of ideas, but the other half of the moral is applied. In Milton's story disobedience makes men miserable, in Lewis's obedience makes the Perelandrans happy. The Green Lady has a real possibility of choice.

> It was suddenly borne in upon him that her purity and peace were not, as they had seemed, things settled and inevitable like the purity and peace of an animal — that they were alive and therefore breakable, a balance maintained by a mind and therefore, at least in theory, able to be lost. There is no reason why a man on a smooth road should lose his balance on a bicycle; but he could. There was no reason why she should step out of her happiness into the psychology of our own race; but neither was there any wall between to prevent her doing so. The sense of precariousness terrified him: but when she looked at him again he changed that word to Adventure, and then all words died out of his mind. [8]

---

[8] Lewis, *Perelandra*, p. 68.

The Unman attempts to persuade her to break the prohibition against spending the night on the Fixed Land. Like the apple in Milton's version of the Genesis story, this is a test of obedience; but it is also symbolic of the nature of the temptation the Unman holds out. The Green Lady and the King have lived from moment to moment, accepting the will of God. Since their world is a paradise, with no threats to them and with many unexpected delights, they can live to the full command of Christ to "take no thought for the morrow." The Unman tempts the Lady to leave this state of perfect trust in God and take command of her own future. As Ransom sees, this temptation is dangerous because it embodies a half-truth. The Green Lady and the King must grow and mature, must begin to make their own choices. But if they begin by ignoring the one prohibition which has been laid on them, begin by disobeying the will of God, they will lose freedom, not gain it. In the same way a young person faced with his first real responsibility may choose apparent freedom by escaping or evading the responsibility, or choose real maturity and real freedom by accepting the responsibility. False freedom chooses the easier way and remains immature; real freedom chooses the harder way and grows.

The Unman's temptation of the Green Lady is more subtle than Satan's temptation of Eve. Rather than flattering her beauty, the Unman gives her a false, overdramatic picture of herself as a tragic heroine, sacrificing herself for the King. Rather than directly tempting her to disobedience, he subtly suggests that God really wants her to disobey and thus grow and mature. But because the Lady is able to resist, the Unman's actions bring about just the opposite of what he had planned. He wanted slavery and misery for Perelandra; he brings about their freedom and happiness. Like Satan, the Unman becomes God's tool.

The closing scenes of *Perelandra* show the King and the Green Lady preparing to take up their destiny as rulers of their planet and parents of their race. When that race has grown and matured, they will gain angelic powers and even play a part in freeing our own demon-occupied and dominated planet. Thus the whole Miltonic or Augustinian version of the story of the Fall can be found in *Perelandra*, but given a new direction, for this is the story of a success, not of a failure.

And yet, with all the theological dimensions of *Perelandra*, how much of it is still simply exciting adventure on a vividly imagined world! When we compare Lewis's descriptions of *Perelandra* with the average science-fiction adventure on new worlds, we are amazed at his inventiveness and descriptive power. The mere conception of the floating islands would be enough for a novel to many writers of science fiction. When we think of the Singing Beast, the caves of crystal in which Ransom recovers from his wounds, the mountain he climbs after his recovery, with its brilliantly imagined flora and fauna, we realize how seldom in stories of other worlds we have ever seen any conceptions which are really new in the way Lewis's are. And they are not only new, but beautiful in a way which, as Stella Gibbons bears witness, can create an actual longing to see and enjoy such scenes.

In the main, then, Lewis's theological framework is the orthodox Christian picture of the Fall. But, in addition, Lewis adds imaginative elements to the background of Christianity. In the space trilogy the angels of traditional Christian theology become beings of a "supermaterial" rather than a "nonmaterial" sort. Their "envelopes" or "photosomes" could, in principle, be detected scientifically. In *Perelandra* we have a development of the role of eldils. Whereas in *Silent Planet* they are mainly the rulers of the "rational animals" of Mars, in *Perelandra* there is already the suggestion that they are the "guiding intelligences" of planets, as in certain medieval theories. In *Strength* "eldilology" is further developed to bring in the medieval theory of the planets and their influence. But, of course, these imaginative details are not matters of primary belief. We will discuss some aspects of their function in the next chapter, but part of the reason for them is simply literary. Milton described heavenly wars in concrete terms (sometimes with incongruous effect, e.g., the cannon of the heavenly army). Dante gave detailed descriptions of the geography of hell. If we are to write about nonmaterial realities in literature, one way (and a way used by the greatest writers) is to give concrete imagery for the imagination to work on, while the intellect separates meaning from imagery.

But aside from these invented details, certain emphases and interpretations mark Lewis's dealings with Christian beliefs, as they marked his dealings with Christian morality. Consider, for example, Lewis's story of the averted Fall in *Perelandra*. How is the Lady tempted; what are the arguments of the Tempter? The basic appeal is the same as that in Genesis: "Ye shall be as gods." But the Unman tempts the Lady with two techniques. First, he attempts to convince her that disobeying a clear prohibition of God is somehow "really" doing what God wants done; that the "growing up," the full maturity of the creature, which God desires for it, can be achieved by disobedience of God's command. Second, he tries to convince the Lady that she must sacrifice herself for the sake of her husband, the King; bring him a gift which, although he does not desire it and would reject it if he had a choice, is somehow "good" for him.

Thus the idea of "being like a god" is made concrete in two ways. Man is to be a god *to himself*, by deciding what is good for him without regard to

145

the will of God; and man is to be a god *to others,* by deciding what is good for them without regard to their own choices or preferences and, again, without regard to God's will for them. Some knowledge of the world, combined with a little reflection, will show that perhaps ninety percent of the harm done in the world by "good" people arises from one or the other of these temptations.

Consider the second temptation. Inquisitors, totalitarian governments, authoritarian parents, domineering spouses are obvious examples. But so are social workers, reformers of all sorts, and (getting close to home) teachers. The leftist who decides that the middle class needs a violent lesson and the rightist who decides the leftist needs a forcible bath and haircut are both often prey to this temptation in a particularly virulent form.

The first temptation is, outside of Christianity, usually not recognized as a temptation at all. This is to be expected. More troubling is the fact that it is increasingly not recognized as a temptation within Christianity.

In *Strength* we find some of the same themes, together with others. The N.I.C.E. plays on both temptations to secure support: the idea that "man must take charge of his destiny," that to secure uncertain future goods we must do things now which are obviously evil; and also the idea that great numbers of people are going to be "done good to," whether they like it or not (e.g., Ivy's husband and the villagers of Cure Hardy).

In all of Lewis's imaginative works, one of the great themes is that to choose God is to choose joy, and to choose anything else, no matter how apparently noble or delightful or wonderful, is ultimately to choose frustration, nothingness, sorrow. Certainly, joyous Christians are nothing new; one thinks of Chesterton, Traherne, Ignatius of Antioch. But they are not especially common in our age (only Robert Farrar Capon comes to mind of living writers). And at any rate, Lewis's emphasis on joy has its own special notes. A quotation from Denis de Rougemont which Lewis uses a number of times in different contexts — "Love ceases to be a demon only when it ceases to be a god" — gives his general attitude to all good things. His attitude is not that "you must cease enjoying that and obey God" (although, of course, this may need to be said at certain times), but rather, "Obey God or you will soon cease to enjoy that, or anything else." He has George MacDonald say in *The Great Divorce*,

> Some mortals misunderstand. They say of some temporal suffering "No future bliss can make up for it" not knowing that Heaven, once attained, will work backwards and turn even that agony into a glory. And of some sinful pleasure they say "Let me but have *this* and I'll take the consequences," little dreaming how damnation will spread backwards and contaminate the pleasure of the sin. [9]

This could, of course, be parodied as "be good and you will be happy," but what Lewis says is more complex than this. To paraphrase things he says on a number of occasions, his message is more like

> Make a serious and constant effort to obey God and you will have struggle and pain, but also moments of joy and peace, and you will be on the right road to happiness. Choose anything other than God's will and however great the pleasure at the beginning you will be on the road to fear, anger, hatred, despair and sorrow.

[9] *The Great Divorce* (New York: The Macmillan Co., 1946), pp. 67-68.

Lewis's most complex attempt to deal with religious issues in fictional form is *Till We Have Faces*. Besides themes already discussed in connection with other works, *Faces* contains insights into the problem of the suffering of the innocent, or apparently innocent. Orual writes her book as a complaint against the gods. What has she done to deserve the treachery of her sister Redival, the triple loss of her sister Istra? — first as a sacrifice to the god of the Grey Mountain; then, when Istra has beyond all expectation survived exposure on the mountain, to apparent madness; and finally to the god of the mountain, first as husband and later as avenger of the betrayal Orual forces her to.

But as Orual writes, and as she goes on living after the completion of the first book of her story, she gradually begins to learn some of the answers to her complaints. She sees how the behavior of Redival is partly due to Orual's turning from Redival to Istra; how her fiercely possessive love of Istra has turned into something monstrous, needing the removal of its object for any hope of cure; how her sufferings have aided Istra and Istra's sufferings have aided Orual. Here things that Lewis argues for in *The Problem of Pain*[10] are given fictional life. But above all, *Faces* shows how pain makes us grow, mature, become "real." As Orual says at the end of her second book:

> When the time comes to you . . . you will be forced at last to utter the speech which was lain at the center of your soul for years, which you have, all that time, idiot-like, been saying over and over. . . . I saw well why the gods do not speak to us openly or let us answer. Till that word can be dug out of us, why should they hear the babble that we think we mean?

---

10 New York: The Macmillan Co., 1943.

How can they meet us face to face till we have faces?" [11]

In sum, then, Lewis's imaginative works reveal a mind which thinks naturally in Christian terms and can give these terms new imaginative life. Those who agree with Lewis will be grateful for seeing ideas which they share expressed in a vivid, imaginative form. But even those who disagree most with Lewis should be grateful to him for giving them a glimpse not only into a Christian mind but also into a Christian imagination.

[11] Lewis, *Till We Have Faces* (Grand Rapids: Wm. B. Eerdmans Publishing Co., 1964), p. 294.

Conclusions

chapter 8

The Baptism of the Imagination

The imaginative fiction of Lewis and Tolkien has various effects on those who read it. Here I will somewhat arbitrarily divide the total effect into parts and discuss each in turn. The first effect for many is that attributed by the Second Voice in "Leaf by Niggle" to Niggle's completed work — "a holiday and a refreshment." In Lewis's Narnia story, *The Voyage of the Dawn Treader*, Lucy encounters in a book of spells a spell "for the refreshment of the spirit."

> But what Lucy found herself reading was more like a story than a spell. It went on for three pages and before she had read to the bottom of the page she had forgotten that she was reading at all. She was living in the story as if it were real, and all the pictures were real too. When she had got to the third page and came to the end she said, "That is the loveliest story I've ever read or ever shall read in my whole life. Oh, I wish I could have gone on reading it for ten years. . . . oh dear, it's all fading away again. . . . How can I have forgotten? It was about a cup and a sword and a tree and a green hill, I know that much. But I can't remember, and what *shall* I do?" And she never could remember; and ever since that day

what Lucy means by a good story is a story which reminds her of the forgotten story in the Magician's Book. [1]

Many of us in reading the fantasies of Tolkien and Lewis have had an experience not unlike that of Lucy.

The next effect ascribed by the Second Voice to Niggle's work is that "it's splendid for convalescence." In relation to Tolkien's work, the convalescence is, especially from the modern view of the world, pointless, absurd, and futile. Because Tolkien's world is not specifically Christian, it can serve as a halfway house for those struggling out of the grayness of the modern view. For Tolkien's view is a world of purpose, a world where there is a real struggle between good and evil, a hope and danger which go beyond the personal. As Lewis says in a review of the *Ring* trilogy:

The value of the myth is that it takes all the things we know and restores to them the rich significance which has been hidden by "the veil of familiarity." The child enjoys his cold meat, otherwise dull to him, by pretending it is buffalo, just killed with his own bow and arrow. And the child is wise. The real meat comes back to him more savory for having been dipped in a story; you might say that only then is it real meat. If you are tired of the real landscape, look at it in the mirror. But putting bread, gold, horse, apple, or the very roads into a myth, we do not retreat from reality, we rediscover it. As long as the story lingers in our mind, the real things are more themselves. This book applies the treatment not only to bread or apple, but to good and evil, to our endless perils, our anguish and our joys. By dipping them in myth we see them more clearly. I do not think he could have done it any other way. [2]

[1] Lewis, *The Voyage of the Dawn Treader* (New York: The Macmillan Co., 1952), pp. 134-35.
[2] Neil D. Isaacs and Rose A. Zimbardo, eds., *Tolkien and the Critics* (Notre Dame, Ind.: University of Notre Dame Press, 1968), pp. 15-16.

Tolkien himself says the same thing in these words: "By the forging of Gram cold iron was revealed; by the making of Pegasus horses were ennobled; in the Trees of the Sun and Moon root and stock, flower and fruit are manifested in glory." [3] Thus it is not only the refreshment of holiday we get while actually reading the story that is important, but the new eyes we bring back to familiar scenes. (The same, of course, is true of any good holiday.)

Lewis can have this effect, too, for those who have no phobia against his basically Christian outlook. (And increasingly, people lack such a phobia by lacking any real knowledge of Christianity.) But for the Christian, Lewis can also have the effect of purging the imagination of inadequate images associated with his beliefs. Thus Lewis's eldils cleanse our imaginations of misleading associations of angels with vapid-looking ladies in pastel bathrobes, or chubby infants with wings. Yet Lewis does not intend to replace one false image of angels with another. No doubt it is an advantage to replace a bad image with a better one, but the point is to be able to get beyond the images — insofar as this can be done, that is. Lewis says in *Letters to Malcolm*,

> Talk of meeting [God] is, no doubt, anthropomorphic; as if God and I could be face to face, like two fellow-creatures, when in reality He is above me and within me and below me and all about me. That is why it has to be balanced by all sorts of metaphysical and theological abstractions. But never, here or anywhere else, let us think that while anthropomorphic images are a concession to our weakness, the abstractions are the literal truth. Both are equally concessions; each singly misleading, and the two together mutually corrective. Unless you sit to it very lightly,

---

[3] *Tree and Leaf* in *The Tolkien Reader* (New York: Ballantine Books, 1966), p. 59.

155

continually murmuring "Not thus, not thus, neither is this Thou," the abstraction is fatal. It will make the life of lives inanimate and the love of loves impersonal. The naif image is mischievous chiefly in so far as it holds unbelievers back from conversion. It does believers, even at its crudest, no harm. What soul ever perished for believing that God the Father really has a beard? [4]

Again, when Lewis makes Christ appear as a magnificent golden lion in the Narnia stories, this helps to get rid of certain silly or puerile ideas of Christ. (Jane Studdock in *Strength* remembers "pictures of Christ, apparently seven feet tall, with the face of a consumptive girl.") But certainly the idea of Christ as a golden lion is not intended to inspire primary belief. Remember that Aslan does not allegorically "stand for" Christ, he *is* Christ as Christ is feigned to be in that world.

An analogy may be useful here. Lewis, in *The Discarded Image*, describes in great detail the medieval world view. This world view "had a serious defect — it was not true." But the point is that there are many world views, and our own present world view may be no truer. Lewis says, "I hope no one will think I am recommending a return to the Medieval Model. I am only suggesting considerations that may induce us to regard all Models in the right way, respecting each and idolizing none. . . . No Model is a catalogue of ultimate realities, and none is a mere fantasy." [5] What Lewis says about "Models," or world views, may be said with equal truth about the images and associations that surround our ideas of God or Christ or angels. Even the much-derided image of God as an old man

[4] *Letters to Malcolm* (New York: Harcourt, Brace & World, 1964), p. 23.

[5] *The Discarded Image* (New York: Cambridge University Press, 1964), p. 222.

with a white beard attempts to convey ideas of venerability, authority, dignity. (In fact, it fails with many moderns partly because we no longer associate dignity, authority, and venerability with age.) Even the pictures of Christ which so repelled Jane Studdock were attempts to convey the mercy and patience which are really present in the gospel picture of Christ.

It might be thought that if all images are to some extent misleading, we should do without images. But this has a curious effect. If we try to think of a purely spiritual being — God, an angel, a disembodied soul — we rightly leave out the ideas of size, shape, weight, color, and so on. But the effect of removing these ideas and putting *nothing* in their place is to leave ourselves with the idea of something thin, gaseous, ghostly. This is not true of everyone, of course; some minds are less dependent on images. But I suspect that even some very able philosophers have been subconsciously influenced by this idea of spirit as something thin and gaseous. The difficulty which so many philosophers have felt about the ability of mind to affect body may, I think, be traced partly to the fact that subconsciously the problem has seemed to be "how can this insubstantial, gassy stuff affect this solid, massive material?" The medieval theory of "animal spirits" which Lewis discusses in *The Discarded Image* (pp. 167-69) is good, indirect evidence of this: animal spirits are an insubstantial sort of matter which can be affected by mind and which in turn can affect body.

Lewis counteracted this danger of thinking that spirit is insubstantial and gaseous by giving us a counterimage, that of spirit as supersolid. The eldils in *Silent Planet* and *Perelandra* are described as being more solid and real than material beings.

What we call firm things — flesh and earth — seem to [the eldil] thinner and harder to see, than our light, and more like clouds, and nearly nothing. To us an eldil is a thin, half-real body that can go through walls and rocks; to himself he goes through them because he is solid and firm and they are like clouds. [6]

This idea is used again in *The Great Divorce*, where the spirits of the blessed in heaven are "Solid People" compared with whom the visitors from hell are thin and ghostly. The result of journeying further into heaven is to grow more and more solid. Lewis also uses the idea of size: "All Hell is smaller than one of your earthly worlds; but it is smaller than one atom of *this* world, the Real World. Look at your butterfly. If it swallowed all Hell, Hell would not be big enough to do it any harm or to have any taste." [7]

By such devices and others, Lewis has managed, at least for some, to make the detestable quality of hell and the desirableness of heaven imaginatively real. Even the hints, which are all we receive in *Screwtape* or *The Great Divorce* about the nature of heaven, get from many of us an imaginative and emotional response out of all proportion to their brevity; and the final chapters of *The Last Battle*, in which the heroes and heroines of the Narnia books go "further up and further in" into Aslan's country, are to my mind one of the best suggestions of heaven in literature. But the great joy of that country is to be with Aslan, and the essential lovableness of Aslan is something which builds up all through the Chronicles of Narnia.

I am not entirely sure how Lewis has accomplished the feat of making a Christ-figure both convincing and lovable, but he has, succeeding where Milton and others as great have failed. I suspect that part of the secret is Lewis's own quiet goodness and devotion to

---

[6] Lewis, *Out of the Silent Planet* (New York: The Macmillan Co., 1965), p. 95.

[7] *The Great Divorce* (New York: The Macmillan Co., 1946), pp. 122-23.

Christ. But from the purely literary and philosophical point of view we can see some of the techniques which Lewis used to build up a picture of Aslan.

Lewis has put Aslan "on stage" sparingly. Of the approximately 1,300 pages in the seven Narnia books, Aslan appears on well less than a third, and his appearance is generally either the climax of the story or some turning point in it. His presence is something special, a great occasion, not everyday life — not yet, at any rate.

The writer did not make the mistake — which would be a very natural one in a children's book — of making Aslan *too* meek and mild. He is an imposing, even sometimes terrifying, figure. As Lewis says in *The Lion, the Witch and the Wardrobe*:

> People who have not been in Narnia sometimes think that a thing cannot be good and terrible at the same time. If the children had ever thought so, they were cured of it now. For when they tried to look at Aslan's face they just caught a glimpse of the golden mane and the great, royal, solemn, overwhelming eyes; and then they found they couldn't look at him, and went all trembly. [8]

When any of the children attempt to lie to Aslan or be less than honest with themselves or him, his growl is terrible. And his strength and power are always in the background: "The Lion shook his mane and clapped his paws together. ('Terrible paws,' thought Lucy, 'if he didn't know how to velvet them!')" (p. 115).

Lewis has made it clear that to be with Aslan is joy, but also that Aslan is capable of sorrow and of being hurt and appreciates his human friends. After

---

[8] *The Lion, the Witch and the Wardrobe* (New York: The Macmillan Co., 1951), p. 117.

Aslan has returned from death, Lewis vividly portrays his joy and power.

> "Oh, children," said the Lion, "I feel my strength coming back to me. Oh, children, catch me if you can!" He stood for a second, his eyes very bright, his limbs quivering, lashing himself with his tail. Then he made a leap high over their heads and landed on the other side of the Table.
>
> Laughing, though she didn't know why, Lucy scrambled over to it to reach him. Aslan leaped again. A mad chase began. Round and round the hilltop he led them, now hopelessly out of their reach, now letting them almost catch his tail, now diving between them, now tossing them in the air with his huge and beautifully velveted paws and catching them again, and now stopping unexpectedly so that all three of them rolled over together in a happy laughing heap of fur and arms and legs. It was such a romp as no one has ever had except in Narnia; and whether it was more like playing with a thunderstorm or playing with a kitten Lucy could never make up her mind. And the funny thing was that when all three finally lay together panting in the sun the girls no longer felt in the least tired or hungry or thirsty. [9]

Aslan never magically solves the children's problems. They must fight and struggle and plan, and finally Aslan will give them help against problems they cannot overcome themselves. For example, he kills the witch and turns the victims she has turned to stone back into flesh. But Peter and Edmund must fight the witch's army, and Lucy must use the medicine she got from Father Christmas to cure ordinary wounds. Lewis shows Aslan as unpredictable, not to be used for the purposes of others: "Mr. Beaver had warned them, 'He'll be coming and going,' he had said. 'One

---

[9] Ibid., pp. 148-49.

day you'll see him and another you won't. He doesn't like being tied down — and of course he has other countries to attend to. It's quite all right. He'll often drop in. Only you mustn't press him. He's wild, you know. Not like a *tame* lion.'" [10]

One minor but very telling point is that Lewis always shows Aslan as behaving in a "lion-like" way; he is never just "a man dressed in a lion skin." Pauline Baynes's illustrations for the Narnia books, with one or two unfortunate exceptions, carry out this idea. The point here is a rather subtle one. I think what Lewis had in mind was this: just as Christ was really man, not just a puppet or mask of God, so if Christ should become incarnate as a great talking lion, He would subject himself to that condition and work within it.

This gives some hint of Lewis's technique — not imitation or allegory, but what he has called, in a very interesting essay, "Transposition." [11] Just as a musical piece written for the piano may sound quite different when transposed for the violin and may reveal new aspects and new beauties, so Christ's life "transposed" to the world of Narnia and the body of a great lion shows us something new about that life. Thus, for example, the fact that Aslan is a lion enables Lewis to express the joy and glory of the Resurrection as a physical "romp."

Aslan in his actions and language reveals his affection for those who are his friends. His praise is an accolade, and his tenderness and love are clear. Yet friendship with Aslan is not easy and must be chosen and struggled for, Lewis shows. Lucy, Aslan's greatest

[10] Ibid., pp. 165-66.
[11] "Transposition" is collected in *The Weight of Glory* (Grand Rapids: Wm. B. Eerdmans Publishing Co., 1949), p. 15.

friend, is asked to perform the hardest tasks. ("That's how I treat my friends," said Christ to St. Teresa in a vision. "Yes, Lord," she said, "that's why you have so few.")

Susan, who has often hesitated and faltered in following Aslan, at last becomes a "dropout."

> "Sir," said Tirian, when he had greeted all these "if I have read the chronicles aright, there should be another. Has not your Majesty two sisters, Where is Queen Susan?"

> "My sister Susan," answered Peter shortly and gravely, "is no longer a friend of Narnia."

> "Yes," said Eustace, "and whenever you've tried to get her to come and talk about Narnia or do anything about Narnia she says 'What wonderful memories you have! Fancy you still thinking about all those funny games we used to play when we were children.'"

> "Oh Susan," said Jill, "she's interested in nothing now-a-days except nylons and lipsticks and invitations. She always was a jolly sight too keen on being grown-up."

> "Grown-up, indeed," said the Lady Polly. "I wish she *would* grow up. She wasted all her school time wanting to be the age she is now, and she'll waste all of the rest of her life trying to stay that age. Her whole idea is to race on to the silliest time of one's life as quick as she can and then stop there as long as she can." [12]

It is always easier to say "May we come with you — wherever you're going?" than to follow all the way to the end. Susan is not necessarily lost completely, but how much she has lost!

And so may we lose much. If Lewis has achieved

---
12 Lewis, *The Last Battle* (New York: The Macmillan Co., 1956), pp. 123-24.

the end he attempted, then the picture of Aslan should be a valuable corrective to some faults the average Christian is all too prone to. If we presume too much on Christ's tenderness, we may remember Aslan's growl. If we find ourselves too much at ease in Zion, we should remember the "He's wild, you know. Not like a tame Lion." But if our picture of Christ grows too stern or gray, we should remember the joy, the wild romp.

All these aspects of Aslan are present in the picture of Christ as we have it in the gospels. His presence is a great occasion "but me you have not always with you." He can be terrible, as when He drove the moneychangers from the temple. To be with Him is joy: "Lord, it is good for us to be here!" He sorrows and wants our companionship: "Could you not watch one hour with me?" His joy is in us after the Resurrection: "Did not our hearts burn within us?" He asks us to bear burdens: "He who would be worthy of me must take up his cross and follow me." He is not "tame" even to his friends: "Get behind me, Satan, your thoughts are men's thoughts, not God's." He is truly man "like us in all things but sin." He is tender to us: "Fear not, little flock." And we must take care to remain His friends: "He who acknowledges me before men, him I will acknowledge before my Father in heaven, but he who denies me before men I will deny him before my Father in heaven."

Of course, the gospel picture is far richer than Lewis's. Richer but more confusing, harder to grasp in one piece. Aslan is only an echo or an image of Christ, but such echoes and images help us to see the Original in a truer light.

Thus, for those who believe in the realities Lewis is expressing in new terms, he has done an especially valuable service. But even for the enemies of that vision of the world or the champions of rival visions,

Lewis has surely done a service. For unless we understand what an opponent loves and why he loves it, we have not made a real start in understanding that opponent. And for understanding this, a poet may be at times more useful than a philosopher.

This leads us to the final characteristic the Second Voice attributed to Niggle's work: "for many it is the best introduction to the Mountains." Here we need to distinguish. An introduction, as we have said, is necessarily not the thing introduced. The quotation which heads the last chapter of Lewis's account of his conversion to Christianity is from St. Augustine: "For it is one thing to see the land of peace from the wooded ridge . . . and another to tread the road that leads to it" (*Confessions*, VII xxi). But to continue the metaphor, unless we see that land from afar and learn to love it, we are not likely to take the road. The reading of works like Tolkien's and Lewis's awakens a certain appetite in us, but it does not satisfy that appetite. It may be that that appetite will never be satisfied, but must be eternally frustrated. It may be, as Lewis and Tolkien believe, that it can be satisfied, that "the Gospels contain a fairy-story, or a story of a larger kind which embraces all the essence of fairy-stories. . . . But this story has entered History and the primary world." [13] The tellers of tales can hardly help us to decide this question. We must turn to philosophy and to history and look at hard and complex questions: could this happen? What would it mean if it did? Has this happened?

This is why we have rejected so strongly the Roses' idea of Lewis's fiction as a "formal apology for Christianity." An apology, especially a "formal" one, must appeal to reason, not merely to imagination or emotion.

---

[13] Tolkien, "On Fairy-Stories" in *Tree and Leaf* in *The Tolkien Reader* (New York: Ballantine Books, 1966), p. 71.

Lewis never confused the two appeals, and we would be wise not to.

Where the subcreator *can* help us is in arousing our interest, engaging our desire. What Tolkien says of the Christian Story, that "there is no tale ever told that men would rather find was true," is simply untrue for many moderns. Because their temper of mind is so widely separated from the world of Christianity, because they are ignorant of it, or worse, because they have distorted ideas of it, the Christian Story simply "turns off" many moderns.

Tolkien attacks this disinterest indirectly, Lewis more directly. The Roses, for example, attacked Lewis's "hierarchical" view of the universe and, indeed, it is a view for which the modern mind has scant sympathy. Lewis, in *The Discarded Image*, says that just as "hardly any battery of new facts could have persuaded a Greek that the universe had an attribute so repugnant to him as infinity, hardly any such battery could persuade a modern that it is hierarchical." [14] But Tolkien, by giving us figures of authority who really command our respect (Gandalf, Aragorn, Elrond, Frodo himself), undermines this modern prejudice. Of course, some critics hate hierarchy more than they like Tolkien, and Tolkien has been taken to task for the hierarchical aspects of his world. But others, I suspect, have begun to learn from Tolkien the meaning of such terms as dignity, venerability, and authority (the same terms, remember, that some of the older images of God tried to convey).

One of Tolkien's most successful efforts of this kind (I do not know whether such efforts were undertaken consciously or simply arise from the whole cast of Tolkien's mind) is the understanding which the figure of Frodo gives us. The idea that A's suffering may

---

[14] *The Discarded Image,* p. 222.

benefit not only A himself, but also B, is one of the most basic in Christianity, underlying not only ordinary Christian life, but also the mystery of redemption. Charles Williams, a friend of both Lewis and Tolkien, celebrated this doctrine and gave it his own peculiar angle in what he called the doctrine of "co-inherence." But Tolkien has given it concrete form in the person of Frodo. Frodo, as we have said, is not a figure of Christ — he is too limited, too imperfect, for that. But he is what every Christian should be, an imitator of Christ, one who carries out or imitates in his limited and imperfect way the redemptive suffering of Christ. The often-quoted words of Frodo to Sam, "It must often be so — when things are in danger: some one has to give them up, lose them, so that others may keep them," are words which apply to soldiers who die for their countries, to martyrs who die for civil rights, but preeminently they apply to Christ. That someone else must pay the price for what I enjoy, that I must accept this sacrifice with love and make it in my turn for yet others, is, says Williams, one of the basic laws of the universe. Seeing Frodo, we learn to understand this.

Seeing Frodo, but also seeing Orual; seeing Ransom on Perelandra, Aslan in Narnia. Lewis has dealt with the theme, too, and more explicitly. I do not know how many have taken the route from Tolkien to Lewis to Christianity, but it seems to me to be a possible route for the imagination to lead and the intellect to follow on. Yet, whether one goes on from Tolkien to Lewis, or goes on at all from Tolkien, I suspect the reading of Tolkien for many has had the same effect that the reading of George MacDonald's *Phantastes* had on the young Lewis.

It was as if I had been carried sleeping across a frontier, or as if I had died in the old country and came alive in the new. For in one sense, the new country was exactly like the old. . . . But in another sense all was changed. I did not know (and was long in learning) the name of the new quality, the bright shadow that rested on the travels of Anodos. I do now. It was Holiness. [15]

The more specific and demanding effect of Lewis's writing on a mind open to conviction may be represented by this quotation from Chad Walsh:

In *Perelandra* I found my imagination being baptised. At the time I was slowly thinking, feeling and fumbling my way towards the Christian faith, and had reached a point where I was more than half convinced that it was true. This conviction, however, was a thing more of the mind than of the imagination and heart. In *Perelandra* I got the taste and smell of Christian truth. My senses as well as my soul here baptised. It was as though an intellectual abstraction or speculation had become flesh and dwelt in its solid bodily glory among us. [16]

So while for some the words of Lewis and Tolkien may be only a "holiday and refreshment" in a meaningless world, for others "it's splendid for convalescence" from the view that the world is meaningless. And for those ready for the journey their work can be "the best introduction to the Mountains," to that great enterprise of "exploration into God" to which Lewis and Tolkien invite us.

[15] *Surprised by Joy* (New York: Harcourt, Brace & World, 1955), pp. 144-45.
[16] Jocelyn Gibb et al., eds., *Light on C. S. Lewis* (New York: Harcourt, Brace & World, 1966), p. 107.

chapter 9

The Christian Intellect

There are a number of ways of arriving at truth, and almost all of them are inappropriate to imaginative writing. Mathematics arrives at proof by calculation and by deductive proof, which are obviously unsuited to works of the imagination. But the appeal of science to observation and experiment or of history to documentary evidence is equally inappropriate to imaginative writing, for such writing makes no claim to empirical truth — the "facts" of imaginative writing are fictional. Argument — by which philosophy establishes truth — can, however, occur in imaginative writing, because an argument in real life, in a work of fantasy, or in a dream, can in each case be judged simply on its merits as an argument. Thus it is possible that a work of imagination should contain arguments worth considering.

In fact, we will find certain arguments are embodied in the imaginative works of Lewis. But to do full justice to the argumentative backing for the ideas embodied in the fictional works of Lewis and Tolkien we will have to look briefly at some of Lewis's nonfictional works, in which he defends the position he shares with Tolkien.

In general, when we defend a metaphysical theory we try to establish certain things: first, that the theory makes sense; second, that there are no decisive arguments against the theory; and finally, that there are strong arguments in favor of the theory. Of course, a religion is more than just a metaphysical theory, but the higher religions at least embody, or consist partly of, such a theory. Thus, in arguing for the truth of the religious and ethical views he shares with Tolkien, Lewis can be regarded as arguing for the truth of the metaphysical theory embodied in Christianity. In this necessarily somewhat brief treatment we will have to confine ourselves to the essentials of this view, and we will regard these essentials as (1) the creation of the universe by God; (2) the redemption of mankind by Christ; (3) the salvation of individual souls.

A view may be challenged as not making sense in various ways. It may be self-contradictory, so vague or ambiguous as to be meaningless, or it may fail to meet some reasonable standards of meaningfulness which apply to any utterance. Lewis was not greatly concerned with or involved with the kind of technical points which have occupied some philosophers about alleged inconsistencies of contradiction in the Christian view (for example the so-called "paradoxes of omnipotence"), although he says something about them in *The Problem of Pain*. Insofar as he was concerned with the whole question of whether Christianity makes sense, Lewis dealt with it by trying to define traditional Christian beliefs as clearly and cogently as he could. His book *Mere Christianity*, a compilation of talks originally given on radio, is one of his best efforts in this direction; but essays printed in other collections deal even more successfully with specific points. [1] As to the sort of challenge to Christianity which argues that by certain standards of meaningfulness religious statements are nonsensical, it usually turns out that the theories of meaningfulness are themselves controversial and embody a rival metaphysical view. At any rate, Lewis was very little concerned with such controversies.

About more direct attacks on religious belief, Lewis had a great deal to say. A modern writer on philosophy of religion has summed up the major modern objections to religion as falling under four main heads: (1) psychological objection, based on the theory that religion is based on wish-fulfillment; (2) a "scientific" objection based on the idea that there can be no adequate evidence for the miracles which seem to be an integral part of the Christian Story; (3) a philosophical objection based on the unverifiability of religious statements; (4) a moral objection based on the problem of evil in a world created by a good God. [2]

The first of these objections Lewis answered in a number of places in his apologetic works, and the argument occurs in recognizable forms in some of his imaginative works also. The basic argument is that belief in God, redemption, or salvation cannot be explained as "wish-thinking," because everyone has wishes on both sides of the matter. That there should be a God who is completely superior to us, who makes demands on us and has plans for us, who holds us responsible for our actions and may punish us, is far from being the desire of many of us, or of any of us in some moods.

When he comes to deal with the possibility of miracles, Lewis's basic arguments take the form of a dilemma. He shows that Hume's famous argument

---

[1] For example, "On Obstinacy in Belief" in *The World's Last Night and Other Essays* (New York: Harcourt, Brace & World, 1960), which deals with misunderstanding about religious belief.

[2] Sten H. Stenson, *Sense and Nonsense in Religion* (New York: Abingdon Press, 1969), pp. 4-5.

against the possibility of miracles begs the question, for Hume is assuming what he is supposed to be proving, that natural laws cannot be suspended. To say that "uniform experience" shows that natural laws are never broken is simply to assume that miracles have never occurred, which is supposedly the point at issue. But it also raises a deeper issue. Experience can never prove the uniformity of nature, since all arguments from experience assume the uniformity of nature, as Hume himself saw. Thus we have what is called "Hume's Problem of Induction": how are any arguments from experience to be justified? There are difficulties about justifying them *a priori*, and if we justify arguments from experience by arguing from experience, we seem to be arguing in a circle. Lewis poses the following dilemma:

> Theology says to you in effect, "Admit God and with Him the risk of a few miracles, and I in return ratify your faith in uniformity as regards the overwhelming majority of events." The philosophy which forbids you to make uniformity absolute is also the philosophy which offers you solid grounds for believing it to be general. . . . The alternative is really much worse. Try to make Nature absolute and you find that her uniformity is not even probable. By claiming too much, you get nothing. You get the deadlock in Hume. [3]

Thus, unless there is another way out of Hume's dilemma (and philosophers have been unable to agree on any alternative), the theist has a reason for believing in arguments from experience, and the nontheist does not. So, far from there being an incompatibility between theism and scientific reasoning,

---

[3] Lewis, *Miracles: A Preliminary Study* (New York: The Macmillan Co., n.d.), p. 110.

scientific reasoning essentially depends on a theistic philosophy. (That this is historically true, Whitehead, among others, has argued.)

Stenson's third point, that religious claims are "meaningless" because unverifiable, is one about which Lewis has nothing special to say. It is perhaps for this reason that Austin Farrer thought Lewis had "dropped out" of the contemporary philosophical debate and could not usefully be recommended to the *philosophically* puzzled undergraduate. Yet I wonder if Lewis was not wise. The verifiability criterion of meaning is now admitted, even by its early defenders, to be impossible to state in a way which does not make it so weak as to admit all sorts of statements which the early positivists wished to exclude as "meaningless," or so strong as to eliminate perfectly acceptable scientific theories. Indeed, the theory — which demands that every "meaningful" statement be either logically true or false, or else provable as true or false by the methods of science — seems to be self-refuting, for the theory itself seems neither to be logically true nor provable to be true by the methods of science.

Thus Lewis, who wrote for the common reader rather than for the professional philosopher, was perhaps under no obligation to enter the somewhat technical discussions about verifiability which agitated philosophical circles during the time he was writing. What he chose to do instead was of more lasting value.

The problem of evil is perhaps the most important difficulty about belief in God for both philosophers and nonphilosophers. Within professional philosophy the most successful counterattacks on those who have posed this problem have been the argument that moral evil is due to man's free will (the "Free-Will Defense"), and the argument that physical evil (pain and suffering) is explainable as a means of bringing about certain states of character which could not exist without pain and suffering (the "Soul-Making Theodicy").

John Hick's recent book, *Evil and the God of Love,* [4] is perhaps the best exposition of this view by a professional philosopher. But Lewis's *Problem of Pain* had given essentially this sort of argument many years before Hick wrote. Lewis's brief book is "popular" in a way in which Hick's book does not attempt to be, but the essentials of the argument are there.

Austin Farrer summarizes Lewis's argument in this way:

> The very constitution of the world opens the possibility of pain. Our own perversity has seized upon it; we have tormented one another, we have poisoned ourselves. Nevertheless, God's "permission" of evil so multiplied is not simply to be accounted for by his respecting our free will. He takes the harms we mutually inflict and overrules them for our good.
>
> The primary function of mental pain, says Lewis, is to force our misdirectedness on our attention. But just as it belongs to our fallen state to be blind to holiness until we suffer the consequences of sin, and blind to a higher good until natural satisfactions are snatched from us; so equally it belongs to our state that we cannot achieve disinterestedness until it costs us pain. Sympathy is made real by the sharing of distress, and martyrdom is the typical expression of devotion to God.
>
> Such is the central answer Lewis gives to the problem he has undertaken to discuss; and it is difficult to deny that it is the distinctively Christian answer. Many other wise things can be said about the endurance of pain, but it is less evident that they arise out of the Christian revelation. [5]

---

[4] New York: Harper & Row, 1966.

[5] Austin Farrer in *Light on C. S. Lewis,* ed. Jocelyn Gibb et al. (New York: Harcourt, Brace & World, 1966), p. 38.

We recognize that some of these points have been made fictionally in *Till We Have Faces*. Is not Orual blind to the selfish possessiveness of her love for Istra, her neglect of Redival, her battening on Bardia — until the loss of Istra, the separation of Redival, and the death of Bardia bring them home to her? Does not Orual's suffering with and for Istra bring her to a state where the god can say to her, "You, too, are Psyche"?

So much for defense of the Christian metaphysical view against attack. Some philosophers might be content to allow the *possibility* of Christian belief, to show that such a belief is not irrational. But Lewis goes further than this; he gives arguments to show that the Christian metaphysical view is not only possible, but true. One of the most original of these occurs in *Miracles:* [6] it has the form which logicians call "disjunctive syllogism." Two alternatives are posed; one is eliminated leaving the other as the only possibility. Lewis argues that either theism is true — that is, God exists — or naturalism, the view that all events are due to mere chance or natural necessity, is true. But naturalism is self-refuting, for if naturalism is true our thoughts are determined by nonrational causes. But no thought determined by nonrational causes is valid, thus naturalism is self-refuting. So only theism remains.

Lewis himself puts the argument in this way:

To understand that logic must be valid is to see at once that this thing we all know, this thought, this mind, cannot in fact be really alien to the nature of the universe. Or, putting it the other way round, the nature of the universe cannot be really alien to Reason. We find that matter always obeys the same

---

6 Lewis, *Miracles: A Preliminary Study* (New York: The Macmillan Co., 1963).

laws which our logic obeys. When logic says a thing must be so, Nature always agrees. No one can suppose that this can be due to a happy coincidence. A great many people think that it is due to the fact that Nature produced the mind. But on the assumption that Nature is herself mindless this provides no explanation. To be the result of a series of mindless events is one thing: to be a kind of plan or true account of the laws according to which those mindless events happened is quite another. . . . But if the validity of knowledge cannot be explained in that way, and if perpetual happy coincidence throughout the whole of recorded time is out of the question, then surely we must seek the real explanation elsewhere. . . . Unless all that we take to be knowledge is an illusion, we must hold that in thinking we are not reading rationality into an irrational universe but responding to a rationality with which the universe has been saturated. [7]

Of course, one might try to show that there is some third alternative between theism and naturalism or try to show that naturalism is not self-refuting. But on the face of it, Lewis has given a powerful argument for theism. To say that this argument is open to objection, and those objections to answers, is simply to say that it is a philosophical argument. As Austin Farrer says, "Philosophy is an evershifting, never-ending, public discussion." [8]

Lewis also gives, in several places, a version of the moral argument for the existence of God. For example, in Mere Christianity he argues that people, when they have moral disagreements, do in fact appeal to common standards of justice. Without such, in fact, standard arguments about moral matters cannot occur.

[7] Lewis, "De Futilitate," collected in *Christian Reflections,* ed. Walter Hooper (Grand Rapids: Wm. B. Eerdmans Publishing Co., 1967), pp. 64-65.

[8] *Light on C. S. Lewis,* p. 31.

Everyone has heard people quarrelling. . . . They say things like "How'd you like it if any one did the same to you" . . . "Leave him alone, he isn't doing you any harm" . . . "Come on, you promised". . . . Now what interests me about such remarks is that the man who makes them is not merely saying that the other man's behaviour does not happen to please him. He is appealing to some sort of standard of behaviour which he expects the other man to know about. And the other man very seldom replies, "To hell with your standard." Nearly always he tries to make out what he has been doing does not really go against the standard, or that if it does there is some special excuse. . . . It looks, in fact, very much as if both parties had in mind some kind of Law or Rule of fair play and decent behaviour or morality or whatever you like to call it, about which they really agreed. And they have. If they had not they might, of course, fight like animals, but they could not quarrel in the human sense of the word. Quarrelling means trying to show that the other man is in the wrong. And there would be no sense in trying to do that unless you and he had some sort of agreement as to what Right and Wrong are. [9]

Lewis answers various objections to the view that there is such a universal moral law and refers to his book *The Abolition of Man*, in which he shows that cultures widely separated in space and time have had essentially the same moral code. Lewis concludes,

It seems, then, we are forced to believe in a real Right and Wrong. People may sometimes be mistaken about them, just as people sometimes get their sums wrong; but they are not a matter of mere taste and opinion any more than the multiplication table. Now if we are agreed about that, I go on to my next point, which is this: None of us are really keeping the Law of Nature. . . . These then are the two points I

9 Lewis, *Mere Christianity* (New York: The Macmillan Co., 1943), pp. 17-18.

wanted to make. First, that human beings all over the earth have this curious idea that they ought to believe in a certain way. Secondly, that they do not in fact behave that way. They know the Law of Nature; they break it. These two facts are the foundations of all clear thinking about ourselves and the universe we live in. [10]

Author Lewis then argues that a materialistic view of the universe offers no explanation of the moral law and our failures to keep it, and the religious view does. The argument is basically an inductive one: here is a fact about the universe — the moral law and our failure to live up to it. Here are competing hypotheses about the universe: the nonreligious view and the religious view. The religious view accounts for the facts, the non-religious view does not. Therefore, by the ordinary standards of inductive reasoning we ought to accept the view which is able to explain the facts — the religious view.

It would be *possible* to argue that the religious view does not explain the facts, but such an argument seems to have little chance of success. It would be possible to deny the facts or argue that they can be explained on purely naturalistic grounds, but we then either deny the existence of the moral law or explain it away. And if we do either, we run up against a serious difficulty. If we want to condemn anything on moral grounds — war, racism, exploitation — we are thereby admitting the existence of moral law, as Lewis has argued. Thus the price we pay for rejecting the religious view is the inability to condemn anything morally. If "that's wrong" means no more than "I don't like that," the man we are condemning can simply reply, "I do like it."

Ordinary people and philosophers have been in-

10 *The Abolition of Man* (New York: The Macmillan Co., 1961), pp. 20-21.

consistent on this point in rather different ways. Ordinary people may be relativists in theory, but try to use the language of moral condemnation when they are really involved or indignant. Philosophers, while often denying in theory the existence of a moral law, appeal to our ordinary judgments of right and wrong to support or criticize philosophical theories about morality. But if A can justify or support B, A must be prior to B.

We may note that the argument depends on the principle, "If objective right and wrong exist, God exists," which is simply the contrapositive of the principle often appealed to by existentialists and others, "If God does not exist, objective right and wrong do not exist." Sartre argues, "No God, therefore no right and wrong"; Lewis argues, "Right and wrong, therefore God." But their major premises are equivalent.

Now neither of the two arguments we have examined is conclusive in the sense that it compels assent. But each argument shows a price we must pay for rejecting theism. The first argument shows that we must either accept the existence of God or deny the validity of human reasoning. The second argument shows that we must either accept the existence of God or deny the validity of any moral judgment. Many people can thus be accused of inconsistency; they try to reject God but at the same time retain reason or morality. But if someone simply denies the validity of reasoning and of moral judgment, then there is no appeal we can make to him — no rational appeal, since he denies reason, and no practical appeal, for he denies morality. Of course, there may be some way out of the dilemmas which Lewis's arguments pose, but he has given us a powerful *prima facie* case.

Another often-encountered argument for religion is the argument from religious experience. Sometimes this argument focuses on mystical experiences which are completely outside the lot of most of us, and it has been argued that someone else's experience, no matter how convincing to him, can never be a sufficient reason for us. But Lewis argues from a religious experience which he feels all of us have had in some form or other. It is an experience of longing, of a desire for joy which in itself is a joy beyond all other joys. This experience is the theme of Lewis's autobiographical *Surprised by Joy* and his autobiographical allegory *The Pilgrim's Regress*. The evidential value of this sort of longing he succinctly expresses in *Mere Christianity*.

> Most people, if they had really learned to look into their own hearts, would know that they do want, and want acutely, something that cannot be had in this world. . . . If I find in myself a desire which no experience in this world can satisfy, the most probable explanation is that I was made for another world. If none of my earthly pleasures satisfy it, that does not prove that the universe is a fraud. Probably earthly pleasures were not meant to satisfy it, but only to arouse it, to suggest the real thing. If that is so, I must take care, on the one hand, never to despise, or be unthankful for, these earthly blessings, and on the other, never to mistake them for the something else of which they are only a kind of copy, or echo, or mirage. I must keep alive in myself the desire for my true country, which I shall not find till after death; I must never let it get snowed under or turned aside; I must make it the main object of life to press on to that other country and to help others to do the same. [11]

As with the previous two arguments, we can reject Lewis's conclusion, at a price. Just as the first argument showed that to reject God is to reject reason, and the second showed that to reject God is to reject

---

[11] *Mere Christianity*, pp. 119-20.

morality, so this third argument shows that to reject God is to reject our hope of real happiness. Unless Lewis is wrong, the result of all three rejections will be, indeed, a grim and meaningless world.

About the other essentials of the Christian world view, redemption and salvation, of course no purely philosophical argument can be conclusive. For we must also examine certain historical evidence about the life of Christ and the history of Christianity. Lewis attacked on two fronts here. As an expert in the history of literature he attacked certain excesses of modern biblical criticism on purely professional grounds. He also argued that, given the record we have of Christ's life, we must conclude either that He was God or that He was a lunatic or an evil man. As Lewis says:

> I am trying here to prevent anyone the really foolish thing that people often say about Him: "I'm ready to accept Jesus as a great moral teacher, but I don't accept His claim to be God." That is the one thing we must not say. A man who was merely a man and said the sort of things Jesus said would not be a great moral teacher. He would either be a lunatic — on a level with the man who says he is a poached egg — or else he would be the Devil of Hell. You must take your choice. Either this man was, and is, the Son of God, or else a madman or something worse. You can shut Him up for a fool, you can spit at Him and kill Him as a demon; or you can fall at His feet and call Him Lord and God. But let us not come out with any patronizing nonsense about His being a great human teacher. He has not left that open to us. He did not intend to. [12]

There is an echo of this argument in *The Lion, the Witch and the Wardrobe*, when Lucy claims to have stepped through the wardrobe into Narnia and the

---

[12] Ibid., pp. 55-56.

others do not yet believe her. They appeal to Professor Kirk.

> "Logic!" said the Professor half to himself. "Why don't they teach logic at these schools? There are only three possibilities. Either your sister is telling lies, or she is mad, or she is telling the truth. You know she doesn't tell lies and it is obvious that she is not mad. For the moment then, and unless any further evidence turns up, we must assume she is telling the truth." [13]

Finally we should take note of an interesting piece of argument which occurs as part of the action in *The Silver Chair*. Eustace and Jill have broken the enchantment on Prince Rilian, and the witch is trying to get all three back under her spell. Lewis has some excellent fun here showing that the same sort of argument which has been used by some to explain away the idea of God and heaven and so on can be used by the witch to deny the reality of anything outside her own underground kingdom. But our main concern is with the speech Puddleglum the Marsh-wiggle makes in reply to the witch's blandishments. (He has just put his foot into the fire to destroy the effect of a hypnotic powder the witch is burning.)

> The pain itself made Puddleglum's head for a moment perfectly clear and he knew exactly what he really thought. There is nothing like a good shock of pain for dissolving certain kinds of magic.
>
> "One word, Ma'am," he said, coming back from the fire; limping, because of the pain. "One word. All you've been saying is quite right, I shouldn't wonder. I'm a chap who always liked to know the worst and then put the best face I can on it. So I won't deny any of what you said. But there's one thing more to be said, even so. Suppose we *have* only dreamed, or

---

[13] Lewis, *The Lion, the Witch and the Wordrobe* (New York: The Macmillan Co., 1951), p. 47.

made up, all those things — trees and grass and sun and moon and stars and Aslan himself. Suppose we have. Then all I can say is that, in that case, the made-up things seem a good deal more important than the real ones. Suppose this black pit of a kingdom of yours is the only world. Well, it strikes me as a pretty poor one. And that's a funny thing, when you come to think of it. We're just babies making up a game, if you're right. But four babies playing a game can make a play-world which licks your real world hollow. That's why I'm going to stand by the play-world. I'm on Aslan's side even if there isn't any Aslan to lead it. I'm going to live as like a Narnian as I can even if there isn't any Narnia. So, thanking you kindly for our supper, if these two gentlemen and the young lady are ready, we're leaving your court at once and setting out in the dark to spend our lives looking for Overland. Not that our lives will be very long, I should think; but that's small loss if the world's as dull a place as you say." [14]

And this, I think, would be Lewis's final answer to any attack on Christianity in the name of modern viewpoint: he knows perfectly well that Christianity is true, just as the children and the Marsh-wiggle know perfectly well that trees and sun and grass exist. But if, per impossibile, Christianity was false, it would still be a bigger view of the universe than that of the materialist. If it were a dream, it would be man's greatest dream. As Tolkien says, "It has preeminently the 'inner consistency of reality.' There is no tale told that men would rather find was true." And just as Puddleglum would be on Aslan's side even if there isn't any Aslan to lead it, live as like a Narnian as he can even if there isn't any Narnia, so Lewis and Tolkien would, I think, want to be on Christ's side even if there isn't any Christ to lead it, be citizens of the

[14] Lewis, *The Silver Chair* (New York: The Macmillan Co., 1953), pp. 156-57.

kingdom of God even if there isn't any kingdom of God.

Indeed, Lewis says in *Letters to Malcolm*,

> Even now, even if — let's make an impossible sup-position — His voice, unmistakably His, said to me, "They have misled you. I can do nothing of that sort for you. My long story is nearly over. I die, children. The story is ending" — would that be the moment for changing sides? Would not you and I take the Viking way: "The Giants and the Trolls win. Let us die on the right side, with Father Odin." [15]

Tolkien, I am sure, would agree. The view of Northern mythology is false; the monsters will not defeat the gods. But if they did, then, as Lewis says in *Poems*,

> the weary gods . . .
> Will limp to their stations for the last defence. Make it your hope
> To be counted worthy on that day to stand beside them
> For the end of man is to partake of their defeat and die
> This second, final death in good company. The stupid, strong
> Unteachable monsters are certain to be victorious at last
> And every man of decent blood is on the losing side. [16]

In summary, then, everything points to the reality of God: reason, morality, the deepest desires of our hearts. The usual objections to belief in God can be answered. Belief is reasonable. But it is also a total commitment of the whole person; better to die with God than live without God.

---

[15] *Letters to Malcolm* (New York: Harcourt, Brace & World, 1964), p. 120.

[16] *Poems,* ed. Walter Hooper (New York: Harcourt, Brace & World, 1964), p. 4.

chapter 10

The Continuing Battle

"All this is very well," it might be said, "but what relevance do Lewis and Tolkien have to the problems we face today?" Now partly this demand for relevance is itself a mistake in the eyes of Lewis and Tolkien; the greatest problems we face are "eternal not temporal." But the objection can be answered, at least partially, in its own terms.

Consider, for example, our modern problems of race. One effect of entering secondary worlds with a number of nonhuman "speaking races" must surely be to make us see that differences in color or culture among human races are fairly trivial differences. People from other cultures or (sometimes) of other races are different from ourselves, but why not rejoice in and enjoy such differences, as Sam the hobbit enjoys elves or as Lewis's Malacandran races enjoy each other.

The sorns in *Silent Planet* find certain things Ransom tells them about earth interesting.

Two things about our world particularly stuck in their minds. One was the extraordinary degree to which problems of lifting and carrying things absorbed our energy. The other was the fact that we had only one kind of *hnau* [rational being]: they thought this must have far reaching effects in the narrowing of sympathies and even of thought. "Your thought must be at the mercy of your blood," said the old *sorn*. "For you cannot compare it with thought that floats on a different blood."[1]

But though we lack differences of the sort which Ransom found on Mars we can perhaps to some extent compare our thoughts with those which "float on a different blood."

Notice that in Tolkien openness and interest in other races are not characteristic of hobbits as such. They are a closed-minded and provincial lot, suspicious even of hobbits who live beyond the Brandywine River or in Bree, to say nothing of elves, dwarves, and wizards. (The Bree hobbits reciprocate by calling the Shire hobbits "outsiders.") It is only Bilbo, Frodo, Sam, Merry, and Pippin who in various degrees are interested in other creatures. And how richly they are rewarded! To put it at its lowest, they have much more *fun*, one would think, than the average hobbit.

Similarly, those in our world who close themselves into their own culture are shutting themselves off from a great deal of enjoyment, if nothing worse. And this fault is not confined to the white "middle American"; some Black, Chicano, and other ethnic groups seem to feel they can appreciate their own cultural heritage only by despising that of others. The truth is that real appreciation for any one race or culture helps you gain real appreciation of all others. Sam and Frodo and the others could appreciate the hobbit virtues after wandering with elves aand dwarves. Ransom returned from Venus and Mars to preside over the peaceful and joyous community at St. Anne's. In our increasingly hard and hateful times it is becoming difficult to appreciate. But it is well worth the effort.

---

[1] Lewis, *Out of the Silent Planet* (New York: The Macmillan Co., 1965), pp. 102-3.

Ecology is another major issue of our times. Lewis's vision of man's original destiny can be seen on Perelandra, where the King and the Green Lady are to rule their planet as God's stewards, enhancing not destroying their environment, helping and guiding the animals instead of abusing them. Tolkien shows us the reverse side of the coin: the Dark Lord blasts and destroys the natural surroundings in and near Mordor; and when Saruman begins to become like the Enemy, he begins to lay waste the area near his tower and destroys trees. In contrast, Legolas delights in the ancient forest of Fangorn, and Gimli is in ecstasy at the beauty of the great caverns below Hornburg.

The students who enjoy Tolkien are awake to this aspect of his work. Recently a construction project on my campus destroyed some grass and trees near the library building, perhaps a necessary but certainly regrettable preliminary to expansion of the library. On the board fence surrounding the project a number of slogans were painted. One near the entrance said simply "The Gates of Mordor." Unfair, perhaps, but Tolkien — who was moved to write "Leaf by Niggle" when a tree near his home was cut down — would have understood.

Another "relevant" aspect of Lewis and Tolkien is their insistence on personal responsibility, on doing what we can (and often more than we want to) in whatever situation we face. Frodo with the Ring and Ransom on Perelandra are obvious examples. The theme of responsibility (and growth through accepting responsibility) is a constant theme in Tolkien and Lewis. Bilbo in *The Hobbit*, Niggle in "Leaf by Niggle," Lucy, Peter, Jill, and Eustace in the Narnia stories all demonstrate the theme. Our own particular responsibility may look quite undramatic, quite unlike the Ring or a quest set by Aslan; but sticking determinedly to a task is a virtue Lewis and Tolkien have managed to make more exciting than most other authors I can think of.

Another aspect of the sort of heroism celebrated by Lewis and Tolkien is that it is preeminently a heroism for hard times and seemingly hopeless situations. Now I would not willingly discourage the faint-hearted, but any hope based on the idea that the problems of our country or our world are likely to be solved without heroism and sacrifice (or even, perhaps, with them) is bound to be disappointed. And a sojourn in the secondary worlds of Tolkien or Lewis is no bad preparation for facing grim situations and fighting for seemingly hopeless causes. As Gimli the dwarf says of the land of the Rohirrim: "There is good rock here. This country has tough bones."

We have seen that Lewis and Tolkien both emphasize the danger of using evil means for even the best ends. As our situation grows more and more grave, this is a temptation to which we are particularly susceptible. The radical who destroys and burns to make a better world or the conservative who uses repression in defense of freedom and order is increasingly characteristic of our time. And increasingly it is becoming difficult for those who use such means to see anything wrong with using them. The purity of their goals and the urgency of their situation increasingly blind them to what they are doing to themselves and others. We live more and more in Mordor, and whichever side wins in any of our tangled controversies, the prospects for ease or peace or freedom are increasingly dim.

The insistence on responsibility in Tolkien and Lewis, the reminders that bad means contaminate the ends they are used for, may seem to be contradicted by the fact that some in the "youth culture" appear to couple an enjoyment of Tolkien, or even of Lewis, with irresponsibility, retreat into the world of drugs, retreat from reality. I think this can be partly accounted for by simple despair. As Lewis says of his life at one point, when his love of fantasy and romance in literature was coupled with a materialistic philosophy, "Nearly everything I loved I thought to be imaginary." This, it seems to me, is the situation of many moderns. They lack Tolkien's and Lewis's belief in realities beyond this world, or the strength which would enable them "to live like a Narnian even if there isn't any Narnia."

Now there is no easy solution for this problem. If the facts about the universe are really such as to warrant despair, then no rhetoric or persuasion is likely to convince some people not to despair. Some people of Stoic temperament will feel pride in demonstrating an "unconquerable soul," but many will simply try to escape or forget in whatever way offers itself. If the universe *is* absurd and futile, then drugs, suicide, an immersion in sex or violence are no more appropriate or inappropriate as responses to it than stoic courage. If there is no basic right and wrong then why should we be impressed by the existentialists' talk of "inauthenticity," for if nothing is wrong, how can it be wrong to be inauthentic?

Again, while many who think the universe absurd and futile have demonstrated nobility and compassion, if any choice is as good as any other, then nobility and compassion are no better as choices than degradation and exploitation of others. The idea that we can retain the essentials of the Christian moral code while rejecting the beliefs which justified that code is an error of the Victorian age which by now should be thoroughly discredited.

We have also disproved, simply by experience, the idea that mere material affluence or a certain kind of social order or any rearrangement of that sort will prove a remedy for the human condition.

John Wain is more clear-sighted than most moderns when he says,

> Naturally I think that human life is tragic. No shallow optimism, no easy faith that humanity will be happy when this or that piece of social engineering has been completed or when we have finished our conquest of Nature. What difference would it have made if my wife and I had met each other on Jupiter instead of Earth? The longest journeys are made within the self. The solitude that can exist within the human mind is more absolute than the emptiness of interstellar space. That is why I care nothing for technology, nothing for science. With all their improvements, they can never touch anything but the surface of human life. The same problems face every man and they always begin again. There are many ways of making life more tolerable, but none of ridding it of its basically tragic quality.[2]

Wain himself finds his vocation as an artist. His desire to create gives purpose to his life. But for those who lack such a purpose, or some parallel to it (Wain recognizes that for some, science is what his art is to him), the outlook that Wain offers can lead easily to despair.

It is true that, with the optimism and idealism of youth, many young people still hope to bring happiness to themselves and everyone by some revolutionary transformation of society. But this is simply another "piece of social engineering," and as Wain recognizes, such changes are no solution to the problems of the human condition.

The alternative that Tolkien and Lewis offer is the Christian alternative. But surely, many will say, it has been tried and found to be no solution. But Tolkien and Lewis would agree with Chesterton that "Chris-

[7] John Wain, *Sprightly Running. Part of an Autobiography* (New York: St. Martin's Press, 1963), p. 262.

tianity has not been tried and found wanting. It has been found difficult and not tried."

But *what* has not been tried? Obviously the world can go very badly, indeed, in places or at times where everyone is nominally a Christian. What *would* make a difference would be a real effort by enough people to make a Christian society and to live a Christian life. But to many of us "a Christian society" or "a Christian life" has very little meaning. Lewis and Tolkien can help us.

Lewis has a brief chapter on "Social Morality" in *Mere Christianity*. He emphasizes that the foundation of any good society is the Golden Rule, "Do as you would be done by." Apart from this,

> Christianity has not, and does not profess to have, a detailed political programme for applying "Do as you would be done by" to a particular society at a particular moment. . . . It was never intended to replace or supersede the ordinary human arts and sciences; it is rather a director which will set them all to the right jobs, and a source of energy which will give them all new life, if only they will put themselves at its disposal. . . . some Christians — those who happen to have the right talents — should be economists and statesmen . . . and their whole efforts should be directed to putting "do as you would be done by" into action. . . . The application of Christian principles, say, to trade unionism or education must come from Christian trade unionists and Christian schoolmasters. [3]

Here we have again the note so frequently in Lewis and Tolkien: the call to personal responsibility. But what would a Christian society be like? Lewis gives us an idea.

---

[3] *Mere Christianity* (New York: The Macmillan Co., 1943), p. 79.

The New Testament, without going into details, gives us a pretty clear hint of what a fully Christian society would be like. Perhaps it gives us more that we can take. It tells us that there are to be no passengers or parasites: if man does not work, he ought not to eat. Every one is to work with his own hands, and what is more, every one's work is to produce something good. . . . On the other hand, it is always insisting on obedience — obedience (and outward marks of respect) from all of us to properly appointed magistrates, from children to parents, and (I am afraid this is going to be very unpopular) from wives to husbands. Thirdly, it is to be a cheerful society: full of singing and rejoicing, and regarding worry or anxiety as wrong. Courtesy is one of the Christian virtues. [4]

In the *Ring* trilogy, we have a sort of illustration of such a society in the Fellowship of the Ring. Aragorn is respected, not only for his royal blood, but for his great knowledge and experience and his long struggle against the Enemy. Gandalf is valued not only for his power but also for his wisdom. These two are the leaders of the party and are respected as such. But their wisdom and experience are at the service of Frodo, the Ring-bearer, and they like and respect Sam, Merry, and Pippin. Legolas and Gimli put their formidable talents fully into the search for Merry and Pippin and are delighted to find them safe.

Similarly, as we have seen, the society at St. Anne's is one where respect, affection, and joy are found together. There is no "swank"; Ivy Maggs is not just *treated* as a full member of the company as a pretense, she *is* a full member. But Ransom is undoubtedly in charge, and his orders are carried out.

This, by the way, may be one reason why idealistic attempts at community, including many contemporary communes, have come to a bad end. There are ex-

---

[4] Ibid., p. 80.

pressions of love and unity, and a good deal of talk about freedom. But without responsibility ("Every one is to work . . .") and respect for each other and for some kind of authority, "love" and "freedom" can come to mean exploitation and freeloading.

Notice, however, that both the Fellowship and the company at St. Anne's have some aspects of a commune. Perhaps a hint that could be taken from them is that each is devoted to a purpose: they got together not merely for the sake of getting together, but to accomplish something worth doing. Groups of civil rights workers in Mississippi, groups of McCarthy campaigners, and peace marchers (as well as soldiers and civilians fighting in wars they believe to be just) report experiences of deep community, and this may be part of the reason.

But lacking a Christian society and lacking opportunities for such specialized communities (as many of us do), there are still many things we can do individually to make society better, including sharing our goods with others. Thus social morality leads us back again to individual responsibility: Christian society can be built only by living a Christian life.

In trying to understand the Christian life, a good place to begin is with that curious trio which struggles over the marshes and mountains to Mordor in Tolkien's Ring trilogy — Frodo, Sam, and Gollum. One of Christ's least popular commandments has always been that which tells us to "love your enemies, do good to them who hurt you." But in Frodo's treatment of Sméagol, the hobbit, who has become Gollum, the monster, we see this commandment at work in a situation we can believe in. Again, Christ's words, "Whoever would be great among you should be the servant of you all," are exemplified in Sam, whose service to Frodo increases his stature to that of a hero and ruler.

Frodo himself, carrying the burden of the Ring, exemplifies the man who "takes up his cross," who remains faithfully despite terrible suffering. Love and forgiveness, humility and service, faithfulness and endurance: these are not all of the Christian virtues, but they are some of the most important.

The solution that Tolkien and Lewis offer to our human problems is difficult. If the universe is meaningless, we may do anything we like; no response is more appropriate than another, and there is no holding to account, no responsibility. Man is on his own, and if he makes a mess of things he will simply die, and that is the end of the story. But if Tolkien and Lewis are right, man has an ultimate and inescapable responsibility. As Lewis says,

> There are no ordinary people. You have never talked to a mere mortal. Nations, cultures, arts, civilization — they are mortal and their life is to ours as the life of a gnat. But it is immortals whom we joke with, work with, marry, snub and exploit — immortal horrors or everlasting splendours. This does not mean that we are to be perpetually solemn. We must play. But our merriment must be of that kind (and it is in fact the merriest kind) which exists between people who have from the outset taken each other seriously — no flippancy, no superiority, no presumption. And our charity must be a real and costly love, with a deep feeling for the sins in spite of which we love the sinner — no mere tolerance or indulgence which parodies love as flippancy parodies merriment. [5]

This is indeed to bear the weight of glory. But the weight we are asked to bear is glorious. The Christian world view of Lewis and Tolkien may be false, and

---

[5] *The Weight of Glory* (Grand Rapids: Wm. B. Eerdmans Publishing Co., 1949), p. 15.

if so we must reject it. But as Tolkien tells us, "To reject it leads either to sadness or wrath."

There is a good deal of sadness and wrath in the modern world. Lewis and Tolkien have tried at least to show us "a more excellent way."

Appendixes

appendix A

Basic Lewis-Tolkien Bibliography

A. Essential Books

TOLKIEN: *The Hobbit*
The Fellowship of the Ring
The Two Towers
The Return of the King
Smith of Wootton Major and Farmer Giles of Ham
The Tolkien Reader

(All available in Ballantine Books paperbacks)

LEWIS: *Out of the Silent Planet*
Perelandra
That Hideous Strength
The Great Divorce
The Screwtape Letters

(All available in Macmillan paperbacks)

The Pilgrim's Regress
Till We Have Faces

(Both available in paperbacks from Wm. B. Eerdmans Publishing Co.)

The Lion, the Witch and the Wardrobe
Prince Caspian
The Voyage of the Dawn Treader
The Silver Chair
The Horse and His Boy
The Magician's Nephew
The Last Battle

(All available in Collier Books paperbacks)

B. Other Important Books

[Inclusion of a book about Lewis or Tolkien implies at least qualified recommendation. Books with useful bibliographies or summaries are noted.]

By Tolkien:

"Beowulf: the Monsters and the Critics." In *An Anthology of Beowulf Criticism*, edited by Lewis E. Nicholson. Notre Dame, Ind.: University of Notre Dame Press, 1963. Paperback.

The Road Goes Ever On: A Song Cycle. Poems by J. R. R. Tolkien, music by Donald Swann. Boston: Houghton Mifflin Co., 1967. Notes by Tolkien.

About Tolkien:

Evans, Robley. *J. R. R. Tolkien*. Writers for the 70's series. New York: Warner Books, Warner Paperback Library, 1972.

Isaacs, Neil D., and Zimbardo, Rose A., eds. *Tolkien and the Critics*. Notre Dame, Ind.: University of Notre Dame Press, 1968. Bibliography. Paperback.

Kocher, Paul A. *Master of Middle-earth*. Boston: Houghton Mifflin Co., 1972.

West, Richard. *Tolkien Criticism: An Annotated Checklist*. Kent, Ohio: Kent State University Press, 1970. Bibliography.

BY LEWIS:

Mere Christianity
Miracles
The Problem of Pain
The Abolition of Man
(All available as Macmillan paperbacks)

The Four Loves
Surprised by Joy
(Both available in Harvest paperbacks from Harcourt Brace Jovanovich)

ABOUT LEWIS:

Cunningham, Richard B. *C. S. Lewis, Defender of the Faith*. Philadelphia: The Westminster Press, 1967.

Gibb, Jocelyn, et al., eds. *Light on C. S. Lewis*. New York: Harcourt, Brace & World, 1966. Bibliography.

Keefe, Carolyn. *C. S. Lewis: Speaker and Teacher*. Grand Rapids: Zondervan Publishing House, 1971.

Kilby, Clyde S. *The Christian World of C. S. Lewis*. Grand Rapids: Wm. B. Eerdmans Publishing Co., 1964. Bibliography, summaries.

Kreeft, Peter. *C. S. Lewis*. Edited by Roderick Jellema. Contemporary Writers in Christian Perspective Series. Grand Rapids: Wm. B. Eerdmans Publishing Co., 1969. Paperback.

Lewis, W. H., ed. *Letters of C. S. Lewis*. New York: Harcourt, Brace & World, 1965. Biographical note by W. H. Lewis.

White, William Luther. *The Image of Man in C. S. Lewis*. Nashville, Tenn.: Abingdon Press, 1967. Bibliography.

ABOUT BOTH WRITERS:

Fuller, Edmund. *Books With Men Behind Them*. New York: Random House, 1962.

Hillegas, Mark, ed. *Shadows of the Imagination*. Carbondale, Ill.: Southern Illinois University Press, 1967.

Huttar, Charles A., ed. *Imagination and the Spirit*. Grand Rapids: Wm. B. Eerdmans Publishing Co., 1971.

Moorman, Charles. *The Precincts of Felicity: The Augustinian City of the Oxford Christians*. Gainesville, Fla.: University of Florida Press, 1966.

Urang, Gunnar. *Shadows of Heaven*. Philadelphia: Pilgrim Press, 1971.

C. Other Sources of Information

COLLECTIONS:

The C. S. Lewis Memorial Collection at the Library of Wheaton College, Wheaton, Illinois, has a fine collection of material by and about Lewis, Tolkien, and related writers, including unpublished letters by Lewis, and unpublished doctoral dissertations on Lewis and Tolkien.

SOCIETIES:

The New York C. S. Lewis Society (Corresponding Secretary: Mrs. Hope Kirkpatrick,

466 Orange Street, New Haven, CT 06511) publishes a monthly newsletter with reports of discussions at their meetings and articles on other information about Lewis.

The Mythopoeic Society (President: Glen Goodknight, Box 24150, Lor Angeles, CA 90024) is devoted to the writings of Lewis, Tolkien, and Charles Williams. It publishes a monthly newsletter and periodically issues *Mythlore*, which contains articles, artwork, and information pertaining to these writers.

D. Of Related Interest

Purtill, Richard L. *Reason to Believe*. Grand Rapids: Wm. B. Eerdmans Publishing Co., 1974.

appendix B

Forerunners and Friends

I begin this discussion of those who have influenced Lewis and Tolkien by raising a question about the importance of influences. Why should we care that A influenced B or that B got a certain idea or image from A? Surely the point is the truth or beauty of the idea or image, not its origin. It seems to me that there are two bad reasons and two good reasons for being concerned with influences.

The two bad reasons are first an overconcern with originality, and, second, a misapplication of the evolutionary idea. Overconcern with originality leads us to make an absurd fuss over who was "really" the first to use an idea or image. For example, pedants are fond of pointing out that Winston Churchill was not the first to use the phrase "iron curtain." But unless Churchill had used it in a famous speech, the phrase would never have gained currency. Or to take a case closer to home, an obscure seventeenth century writer used the idea of letters from a devil for political purposes. But this does not take away the genuine originality of *The Screwtape Letters*. In fact, the "who was first" syndrome like the "which is biggest, tallest, longest" syndrome is simply an idiosyncrasy of our time.

The second bad reason — the misapplication of the evolutionary idea — supposes that there is something like an evolutionary development in ideas, that the better is always later and always develops from the earlier. But if this is true at all, it is true in a very qualified way. What we more often find is a much more complex situation, as any history of philosophy or literature will show. The best may come first, to be followed by misunderstandings or weak imitations. The latter may develop from the earlier or in defiance of it, or by a happy misunderstanding of an earlier view, or in many other ways. Thus, if we expect to find a steady straight-line development, we will be baffled.

But this brings us to the first good reason for studying influences. Sometimes but not always, the study of those who have influenced, or even those who have been influenced by, an author will help us to understand things which we might not otherwise understand about that author. Where the author is obscure or difficult to understand because of distance in time or difference in culture, then such help may be very valuable. I think, however, that Tolkien and Lewis are in most cases understandable enough without such aid.

The second good reason is simply that such information is interesting. If I admire B, I may be very interested in finding that he admired A. This may or may not lead me to admire A, but it might nevertheless be a fascinating piece of information. Thus, for example, I find it interesting although not particularly useful or illuminating to know that Thornton Wilder's novel about Caesar, *The Ides of March*, was almost certainly influenced by Edith Hamilton's *The Roman*

Way. Such interest is perhaps akin to the interest we feel in gossip, but may be no worse for that.

With these preliminaries, let us investigate what authors have influenced Tolkien and Lewis, and in what ways. Two authors frequently mentioned are William Morris and George MacDonald. Lewis has put his debt to both authors on record. He edited a collection of excerpts from MacDonald (*George Mac-Donald, an Anthology*, London: Geoffrey Bles, 1946) and used MacDonald as a figure in *The Great Divorce*. Lewis's admiration for Morris is recorded in an essay, "William Morris," collected in *The Literary Essays of C. S. Lewis*. Tolkien speaks with admiration of Mac-Donald in his essay "On Fairy-Stories," but does not mention Morris. Interestingly enough, there are a number of parallels between Morris's work and Tolkien's. Morris, like Tolkien, created a secondary world of knights and swords, wizards and magic. It was set in a vaguely medieval world, but Morris's Middle Ages were a never-never land with little relation to the real medieval period. Morris was also subjected to criticisms rather like the criticisms of Tolkien we discussed in Chapter 2, and Lewis's defense of Morris could stand equally as a defense of Tolkien.

The question about Morris' style is not whether it is an artificial language — all endurable language in longer works must be that — but whether it is a good one. And it is here that sheer ignorance begins to play its part. I cannot help suspecting that most of the detractors when they talk of Morris' style are really thinking of his printing: they expect the florid and the crowded, and imagine something like Sidney's *Arcadia*. In fact, however, this style consistently departs from that of modern prose in the direction of simplicity. Except for a few archaic words — and since the appearance of the S.O.E.D. it is a pleasure to be sent to the dictionary — it is incomparably easier and clearer than any "natural" style could possibly be, and the "dull finish," the careful avoidance of rhetoric, gloss, and decoration, is of its very essence. Those who are really repelled by it after a fair trial are being repelled not by its romanticism but by its classicism, for in one sense Morris is as classical as Johnson. Long ago, Mr. Alfred Noyes noticed the self-imposed limitation under which Morris describes nature whether in prose or verse — the birds that are merely "brown," the sea that is never anything more remarkable than "blue" or "green." Morris, in fact, obeys the doctrine of generality; he does not number the streaks on the tulip but "exhibits in his portraits of nature such prominent and striking features as recall the original to every mind." That such "just representations of general nature" can, as Johnson claims, "please many and please long," his own writing, and that of Morris, will prove.

> "I sat down on a bank, such as a writer of romance might have delighted to feign. I had, indeed, no trees to whisper over my head, but a clear rivulet streamed at my feet. The day was calm, the air was soft, and all was rudeness, silence and solitude."

> "The road was rough that day, and they went not above a foot-pace the more part of the time; and daylong they were going up and up, and it grew cold as the sun got low, though it was yet summer."

The first sentence is from Johnson and the second from Morris. There are a dozen differences between them, but there are two important similarities; both are content with recording obvious facts in very general language, and both succeed so that we really taste the mountain air. It is, indeed, this matter-of-factness, as Clutton-Brock pointed out, which lends to all Morris' stories their sober air of conviction. Other stories have only scenery: his have geography. He is not concerned with "painting" landscapes; he tells you the lie of the land and then you paint the landscapes for yourself. To a reader long fed on the almost botanical and entomological niceties of much modern fiction — where, indeed, we mostly skip if the characters go through a jungle — the effect is at first very pale and cold, but also very fresh and spacious. We begin to relish what my friend called the "Northernness." No mountains in literature are as far away as distant mountains in Morris. The world of his imagining is as windy, as tangible, as resonant and three-dimensional, as that of Scott or Homer. [1]

But Tolkien need not have learned this generalizing style from Morris. Both were influenced by Northern saga and Old English literature, though Tolkien's knowledge of it is that of a scholar — Morris's that of an amateur.

The contrast between Morris and Tolkien in other respects is interesting. In Morris we find no great struggle between good and evil, but rather personal and somewhat aimless adventuring. There is a certain amount of sex and sensuality in Morris, mild enough now, but extremely uninhibited for the Victorian era in which he wrote. There is something remote and rather impersonal about him. Lewis spoke of Morris's "pastel colors," but I would rather use the image of small, gaily colored figures seen at a distance in space; clear but small. All of this, of course, is unlike Tolkien.

The sense of "geography" which Lewis points out in Morris is equally strong in Tolkien, however, and in other respects there is a closeness of atmosphere in Morris and Tolkien despite the differences. Put it this way: Frodo or Bilbo would not be totally out of place in Morris's world, nor would Raymond or Birdalone feel completely lost in Middle-earth.

Comparisons with MacDonald are harder to make.

---

[1] "William Morris" in *The Literary Essays of C. S. Lewis* (New York: Cambridge University Press, 1969), pp. 220-21.

Lewis's "religious" fantasies are both much better written and more successful as presentations of a Christian imagination than MacDonald's fantasy novels *Phantastes* and *Lilith*. Lewis has, I think, learned nothing about writing or about fantasy from MacDonald. In "straight" religious writing, Lewis may have learned more. In his *Unspoken Sermons* and in the sermons and reflective passages in his potboiling novels, MacDonald explains and illuminates Christian doctrines with extraordinary clarity and beauty. The "holiness" which Lewis found in *Phantastes* is hard for me to see there, but it is easy to find, buried under Gothic absurdities, in such long-forgotten Mac-Donald novels as *A Country Parish* or *Robert Falconer*.

Tolkien shows no signs of being affected by this side of MacDonald, though I think some of it affected him indirectly through Lewis. The atmosphere of *Phantastes* and *Lilith* is quite different from that of Tolkien's books. But MacDonald's children's classics, *The Princess and the Goblin* and *The Princess and Curdie*, are much more like Tolkien; in fact, *The Hobbit*, with its "goblins" (not yet "orcs") underground, and other similarities to MacDonald may have been directly influenced by the Curdie books, or at least by *The Princess and the Goblin*. Tolkien says of MacDonald,

> The Magical, the fairy-story, may . . . be made a vehicle of Mystery. This at least is what George Mac-Donald attempted, achieving stories of great power and beauty when he succeeded, as in *The Golden Key* (which he called a fairy-tale); and even when he partly failed, as in *Lilith* (which he called a romance).[2]

Thus Lewis may have learned something of doctrine and its presentation from MacDonald, and Tolkien

---

[2] *Tree and Leaf* in The Tolkien Reader (New York: Ballantine Books, 1966), p. 26.

may have learned something from Morris about making secondary worlds and about a "generalizing" style. But neither influence is certain, and in both cases Lewis and Tolkien could have learned the same lessons elsewhere.

A clearer influence on both Lewis and Tolkien was G. K. Chesterton. Neither resembles Chesterton much in style; indeed, Chesterton's extravagant, exuberant style was *sui generis* both in fiction and in exposition. But in ideas there was a great deal of influence. Both Tolkien and Lewis quote and mention Chesterton with respect. In addition, a sound Chestertonian can detect Chesterton's ideas at work in many places in both Lewis and Tolkien. Both, I think, would acknowledge Chesterton as one of their teachers, one who taught them to see or appreciate things they would not have seen without him.

But this kind of influence, though it may be the most important personally, is the most "transparent," the least useful for understanding Lewis or Tolkien. They have made his ideas their own, and for that very reason they express them clearly and easily. Thus, whether we encounter an idea first in Chesterton or in Lewis or Tolkien matters little: if it is a good idea we can appreciate it equally in any of the three. Often, too, it may be the case that Lewis and Tolkien say Chestertonian things because their own beliefs or attitudes are similar to his, or because they have arrived at the same ideas independently.

Another important influence on Lewis, and perhaps indirectly on Tolkien, was Charles Williams. He was a contemporary and friend who, during the war years, taught at Oxford and was a member of the group of friends who met regularly in Lewis's rooms there. Williams wrote seven fantastic novels in which magic and the occult form the basis of his "secondary world," in the same way that legendary prehistory forms the basis of Tolkien's and the planets and their inhabitants form the basis of Lewis's. He also wrote plays and poetry as well as books on literary criticism which he himself regards as potboilers.

Williams had a charismatic personality and tended to have disciples rather than friends or students. But in Lewis and Tolkien he met men who were at least his equals in personality and intellect. There was no question of their becoming his disciples, but they became his friends, and the friendship was evidently a very warm and close one, especially on the part of Lewis.

Some writers have seen Williams as the center of the Lewis-Tolkien circle (for example, Charles Moorman in *Precincts of Felicity*). That the circle existed long before Williams came to Oxford and survived years after his death (until Lewis moved to Cambridge, in fact) is one piece of evidence against this view. Moorman notes that Tolkien himself (and his son Chr.stopher, an oftimes member of the circle) saw Lewis as the center of the group.

I think Lewis might have said the group had no center, only a circumference: it was like a group of people seated in a circle, each looking at and talking to all the others — not like a group of disciples clustered around a master at the center of the group. But, to continue the metaphor, Williams's accession made the circumference larger; there was one more person to contribute to the circle and receive from it.

With regard to the creation of secondary worlds or to the craft of writing, Williams had more to learn than to contribute. His last novel, which had the benefit of the group's criticism, is technically better than any of his others.

He contributed more, perhaps, in the realm of ideas. Williams had a genuinely original, if somewhat undisciplined, mind. His theological insights, as expressed in his novels and plays as well as in essays and books on theology, are often exciting. But his style is baroque and sometimes confusing. Lewis — whose beautifully clear mind could extract meaning from prose far worse than Williams's and make order out of material even more scattered and diverse than the ideas broadcast throughout Williams's plays, novels and essays—found Williams fascinating. Tolkien, from the scattered evidence available, liked Williams personally, but was unimpressed by him intellectually.

With Williams we have mentioned the last of the individual authors who had really strong intellectual influence on both men, at least so far as their published testimony is concerned. The rest is speculation. We can find plenty of material for speculation, of course. Lewis, for example, mentioned his enjoyment of Edith Nesbit's children's stories, and I think I can find some influence of the Nesbit books on the Narnia stories. The Phoenix, in *The Phoenix and the Carpet*, may have contributed to Lewis's idea of Aslan; the characters of Peter, Susan, Eustace, and Lucy may have been suggested in some respects by various Nesbit children. Much more speculatively, I wonder if Lewis was not slightly influenced by Arthur Ransome's *Swallows and Amazons*, especially in the character of Susan.

Tolkien is familiar with a great number of fairy tales from many nations, and their influence can probably be discerned at many points in his books. The influence of *Beowulf*, *Gawain*, and other early English stories on Tolkien is also obvious. But what else Tolkien read, for pleasure or instruction, is not easy to discover.

The influence of Norse mythology on both authors is clear (and to a lesser extent of Greek mythology). Both Lewis and Tolkien, of course, were influenced by biblical authors (Tolkien translated the Book of Job for the English version of the Jerusalem Bible) and by many great Christian writers of the past. Lewis was fond of Dr. Samuel Johnson, and one suspects that Johnson would be congenial to Tolkien, too. But Tolkien has not told us.

Of their contemporaries, Owen Barfield, for many years a lawyer, was a member of the circle who met in Lewis's rooms when his work permitted. He was an anthroposophist, and Lewis's own views on many things were clarified by arguing with Barfield. Lewis dedicated a book to him with the inscription: "Opposition is true friendship." Did he also influence Tolkien? Dorothy Sayers was a friend of Lewis and also of Charles Williams. Did she know Tolkien? Such questions cannot be answered, for Tolkien has not told us.

And after all, what does it matter? Lewis and Tolkien are gloriously themselves, whatever they may have learned from others. Let us thank God for them, and enjoy them.

index